Dedicated to

Andy Griffith

June 1, 1926 – July 3, 2012

One of the South's greatest storytellers

from Mount Airy, North Carolina

Southern Fried Ramblings

With Grits and All the Fixins

A 21st Century Cultural Buffet of Dixie's Intellectual Delights

THE REBEL MOUNTAIN
READER II
(Revised)

By Mark Vogl
The Rebel Mountain Storyteller Extraordinaire

Southern Fried Ramblings
With Grits and All the Fixins

By Mark Vogl

©2013 Mark Vogl

First Printing

The Scuppernong Press
PO Box 1724
Wake Forest, NC 27588
www.scuppernongpress.com

Cover and book design by Frank B. Powell, III

All rights reserved. Printed in the United States of America.

No part of this book may be reproduced or transmitted in any form or by any means, electronic or mechanical, including photocopying, recording, or by any information and storage and retrieval system, without written permission from the author and/or publisher.

International Standard Book Number ISBN 978-0-9898399-2-1

Library of Congress Control Number: 2013951979

Table of Contents

Foreward v

Introduction vii

Section I Modern Politics and Culture 1

The South is Right! 3

The Old South's conservative ideology important to the 2012 election 5

The Secession Clock 6

Why are Confederates taken for granted? 8

Southern media spin about Dixie hurts the South 11

Christmas on Rebel Mountain, Texas 13

A Yankee I would listen to — Jed Marum 14

Cross over the River — A Confederate Collection wins Album of the Year 15

As You Were! Citadel Cadet Stories from the Past by Ted Childress 17

Confederate War College moves Secession Clock up one hour 19

Do Southern Democrats embrace their party's rejection of God? 20

Let's outline a new national second political party called Dixiecrat! 22

Section II The Confederate Battle Flag as a Symbol of the South 27

The Rebel Flag has orbited earth, did you see it? 29

Why is there so much hatred towards the Confederate Battle Flag? 30

Never more relevant; never more important 32

Section III The Southern Movement Today 35

50 to 80 million Americans are descendants of a Confederate soldier! 37

What is the South in today's time and place? 38

Battle rages in central Virginia, echoes of the Civil War 41

Is there a Southern movement? Part I 43

Is there a Southern movement? Part II 57

How does the South reclaim its Legacy? 63

Section IV Scotland and Secession at the Turn of the 21st Century 73

Secession is not unique to America! 75

Scotland highlights the fragility of old empires in the 21st Century 76

And the beat for an independent Scotland goes on! 78

Section V Modern Assets and Challenges for the South 81

The Internet is a new avenue to recreate the South … Dixie! 83

Confederate History Month symbolizes continued culture war 85

Confederate Flag and causes of secession collide with 2012 election 86

The Rebel Flag, a failed lesson in citizenship! 91

The Sons of Confederate Veterans have a role in modern America 94

Section VI   The Sesquicentennial 2010 – 2015 97

In the Sesquicentennial, the story of the South should be boldly told. 99

Who owns January 19? 101

Let's create a Confederate holiday 103

The Trans-Mississippi Theater … the unknown Civil War.. 104

History seeks a benefactor.. 106

Dixie's greatest secret 109

Section VII   The Confederate Constitution 111

Answers to today's problems found in third American Constitution 113

Democracy … Southern Style 116

The Confederate Constitution 123

— *iii*

Foreword

If we view the South as an antebellum home, *Southern Fried Ramblings With Grits and All the Fixings* would be the grand entrance of that stately home. The very act of approaching the home is filled with hints of greater things to come. And just like the South, both past and present, the home is filled with many rooms and very interesting people.

Unfortunately in today's politically correct (p. c.) world, most people are fearful of taking the time to investigate the old structure. If the modern purveyors of history and culture had their way, the old structure would be taken down and the lot filled with a collection of fast food establishments or a Walmart parking lot. How is it that the section of this nation which gave us George Washington, Patrick Henry, Thomas Jefferson and a host of other such luminaries is now little more than the butt of p.c. jokes? At one time the United States military named weapons of war and military bases in honor of Confederate officers, even highways in the North were named in honor of political and military heroes of Dixie. Yet, today no military band dares play *Dixie* and the Confederate Flag is forbidden on military bases. In a land where every ethnic group has rights and their culture is embraced and supported, Southern culture is considered an abomination.

With its rich tradition of religious faith, the South understands that evil has and does exist in the South. Our religion teaches us that all men are sinners. General Lee, the most revered Southerner of all men, once told an acquaintance, "I am nothing but a poor lost sinner, trusting in Christ only for salvation." Lee understood the sinful nature of man just as most Southerners still do. Therefore, Southerners have little trouble accepting the fact that evil does exist in our part of the country. Regardless of how Southerners feel about innate evil down South, that in no way absolves other sections of the country from equal guilt for the "sins of the nation." Yet, this seems to be the p.c. pattern when dealing with most problems in which guilt can be laid upon the South — the North is virtuous, the South is depraved.

In his latest book Mark Vogl has given us a chance to look beyond the p.c. hype of an evil wicked South and see a land of freedom, family and friends. Not only are we given a tour (in some cases a *tour de force*) of the foundations of real American liberty, we are given a chance to look into the heart of a people who love each other and desire only to lead their life unencumbered by big government.

Today America is spending itself into total bankruptcy; bureaucratic rules have the full force of law; the will of the people of the States are trampled upon by an all powerful Federal government, and no one seems capable of controlling this ever growing leviathan of big government. After the close of the War for Southern Independence, Lord Acton inquired of General Lee as to the future of the new American government. In response to Lord Acton's question General Lee stated he had great fear for the future if all the rights which once belonged to the States were consolidated into one all powerful central government. Lee noted that once the Federal government became supreme in all matters, it would become "aggressive abroad and despotic at home." What most Americans and sadly most Southerners don't understand is that more was surrendered at Appomattox than just the Army of Northern Virginia. The Declaration of Independence with its demand of the right of the people to "alter or abolish" government; the Constitution which limited the Federal government and with its Ninth and Tenth Amendments reserving *ALL* undelegated rights to "we the people" of sovereign States; and the ability of the people of the States to force the Federal government to abide by the Constitution — all were surrendered at Appomattox.

Let us hope with the publication of Mr. Vogl's latest book, more Americans will understand what was truly lost on that sad April day in 1865 and rededicate ourselves to reclaiming our lost estate of liberty. The motto emblazoned upon the Confederate Battle Flag from King's Mountain, South Carolina, tells the story every American in general and every Southerner in particular should embrace: "Like Our Ancestors, We Will Be Free!"

— *Walter D. Kennedy*

◈ Introduction ◈

Southern Fried Ramblings With Grits and All the Fixins is primarily a compilation of select articles (some modified) from my column, *America Today*, published on Nolan Chart at www.nolanchart.com. However, Section VII features essays concerned with the Confederate Constitution.

This collection of columns stands alone as a modern review of the *Southern nation* and people today. It is not about history, but about today. It is not just about politics but about Southern culture and entertainment.

This work concentrates on the South today, and is primarily about how Southern and Confederate history and values mirror today's world. The essays articulate theories I have developed over a lifetime. It is a central premise of this work that the Southern view of the Constitution in the mid-nineteenth century is a political prescription for the challenges we face today. The book is composed of 33 essays, divided into seven sections:

Section I   Modern Politics and Culture

Section II   The Confederate Battle Flag as a Symbol of the South

Section III   The Southern Movement Today

Section IV   Scotland and Secession at the Turn of the 21st Century

Section V   Modern Assets and Challenges for the South

Section VI   The Sesquicentennial 2010 – 2015

Section VII   The Confederate Constitution

One of the most important theories espoused throughout is the Confederate Founding Fathers, who led the secession movement in 1860 anticipated many of the problems the United States of America faces in 2013 and constructed a Constitution to resolve the problems before they ever rose to the crisis dimensions of today.

Throughout the essays in this book you will see there is a widespread loosely organized modern-day Southern movement. There is no central unifying cause or hierarchy, but rather vague, undefined commonalities which facilitate a degree of cooperation and mutual interest. Cooperation is mostly facilitated by individuals who belong to one or more Southern heritage and Southern political groups and social networks on the Internet like Southern Heritage News and Views and Southern Nationalist Network

But there is more to this book. There is good Southern fun in the form of storytelling. The South is known for many things, and one which is not mentioned very often anymore is the ability of a Southerner to tell a yarn. In 2012 one of the South's most famous storytellers, Andy Griffith, crossed over the river. There will never be another like him. From Andy I learned how to weave a moral into a story, and I hope some of him is in *Southern Fried Ramblings With Grits and All the Fixins*. Though I admit, I am not as subtle or as humorous as Andy.

So get yourself some iced tea, find your favorite chair, kick off your shoes, and set yourself down to wander to places in today's Southland.

May God bless you,

Mark Vogl
The Rebel Mountain Storyteller
Upshur County, Texas

 Section I

Modern Politics and Culture

The South is Right!

The Old South's Conservative Ideology Important to the 2012 Election

The Secession Clock

Why are Confederates taken for granted?

Southern media spin about Dixie hurts the South

Christmas on Rebel Mountain, Texas

A Yankee I would listen to — Jed Marum

Cross over the River, a Confederate Collection wins Album of the Year

"As You Were! Citadel Cadet Stories from The Past,"
by Ted Childress

Confederate War College moves Secession Clock up one hour

Do Southern Democrats embrace their party's rejection of God?

Let's outline a new national second political party called Dixiecrat!

THE SOUTH IS RIGHT!

150 years after the great divide in America, reality seems to be proving that the South was right on everything but slavery, let's look!

The Kennedy brothers, Donnie and Ron shook bookstores across the land when their book *The South Was Right!* boldly proclaimed a view which asserts the original founders of America were right, and Lincoln and the progressives were wrong!

The Kennedy twins are intelligent, educated, successful Southerners who focused their intellects on researching the politics and economics of the antebellum era and found considerable evidence that the South was right. It's a terrific book available at Barnes and Noble, and if you are an American who believes in God, the original founders of America and Declaration of Independence, then *The South Was Right!* should be in your library.

Now, before we go further, let's do what we have to do, condemn slavery as the sin of the past. It was wrong. It was wrong in the North, and wrong in the South. Taking a man's liberty is taking a gift from the Almighty Father and that is wrong. No point wasting a lot of space in debate or discussion. So let's move on.

This article is not about the past; it is about today. It is about an America seemingly in cardiac arrest. It is about an America over-regulated, over-taxed, over-governed. It is about present-day fashions and trends crushing the spirit of liberty which made us America. Our nation is headed in the wrong direction and the markets, and our economy, know it. We need a new direction, and that direction can be found in the history and heritage of the South.

The division in America started almost before the Constitution was dry. Justice Abel P. Upshur, of Virginia, wrote a treatise on the Southern interpretation of the Constitution. Within that work Upshur points to God as the author/creator of sovereignty. Sovereignty is handed from God to man. From man, sovereignty is passed to the states. And it is the states who share a small portion of sovereignty with the federal government. The federal government is last, not first, and the Constitution is a leash to restrain the natural inclination of men in power to seek more power.

Let's start with the beginning. The South, Dixie, is also known as the Bible Belt. 150 years ago, in the Preamble to the Confederate Constitution, the Southern founding fathers called on God for His protection and His guidance. God was invited to the "governing table." This was not something new in America, but it was one of the things the North was changing and the South wanted to keep. If you read *Forged in Faith* or *The Christian Life and Character of the Civil Institutions of the United States* you will discover Christ had been with America since before its conception. Christ and the church were with each of the colonies as they were discovered and settled. Christianity was at the heart of the laws, at the core of the spirit of the people who made the venture from Europe to America. Christ was about liberty, the rule of law, consent of the governed and majority rule. Sovereignty came from God. God is sovereign.

From Him all authority flows.

Many of today's writers on this subject credit the Pilgrims and Massachusetts with using the Bible, and Higher Law to write the Mayflower Compact and plant the seeds for American democracy. The separate religious faiths of Christianity and the pulpit were critical to the foundation of America. The first cohesiveness of America, the first spirit of unity among the colonies came from a mutual belief in a Christian God. All believed God had brought us to America, and that God was in charge.

The North is portrayed as the original Bible Belt. Yet something happened. The North has moved away from God. Today, the South has not. Barack Obama as president has declared we are not a Christian nation. That may work in New York or with the mainstream media, but it doesn't set well if you live south of the Mason-Dixon Line or in the Heartland. America is Christian today. We do believe in the Bible. We do believe in Christ. Our morality, our sense of right and wrong, come from the Higher Law. Everything that America can be stems from this starting point. Everything man can be emanates from the understanding that God exists, that the Bible is His word.

This is not past. This is today. This is the South. Go in its towns. Go to its churches. Talk to people. Listen. The South is not conservative because it has less colleges or universities. The South is not conservative through some genetic fault. The South is conservative because the root of conservatism is a Christian God. It is a belief in something other than government. It is a belief in the partnership between God and man. The South is right!

Since Eden, man has wrestled with the questions of right and wrong. There's no need to. God outlined right and wrong. Like a loving parent He wrote a letter to mankind in the form of the Bible. It tells us right and wrong. No secrets. Nothing scientists have to discover. Nope. Like the basic laws of physics, right and wrong do *NOT* change. Yet, so much of man's energy is wasted in the ebb tides of morality. Yet like gravity or magnetism, right and wrong are consistent, not changed or altered by man.

The South is this place. It is a place where the anchor of God sets the table. While other parts of the nation or people within the nation may chide the South for being the Bible Belt, we wear that description knowing Christ told us we should endure in living His word.

But the South is about much more than its bedrock faith.

The South is about American values. It is about federalism, states' rights and local control. It is about the people in the local area having the most to say about governing themselves. The South is about limiting federal government. The South is about limiting the benefits of working for the government! The best and brightest should not be in government. They should be in medicine, or inventing new technologies, or creating new business formations, or caring for the land and resources of a region.

The South is about capitalism. It is about competition. The right to work is a Southern concept, and unions are seen as a socialist tool to organize workers. Unions have become their own political parties, their own sources of power. Unions do not represent their members. What American jobs did unions fight for? Unions are internationals, not American. They are not Christian; they are secular. Unions are myopic; they are manifestations of cumulative greed seeking power and advantage for a small set of people. And because the South rejected unionism, and wealthy investors poured their monies into the North and not the South, the South was spared the natural inflation which comes with unions.

The South is about understanding that wealth is not money. Wealth is in the land, in the family, and in the things we produce. Money is a tool, not a source of value.

The South is about pride in one's hometown and region. The South is about a regional identity and unity. It is about a way of thinking, a way of singing, and a way of enjoying life. What other region in America has a symbol equal to the Confederate Battle Flag ... a symbol internationally known and respected, a symbol in opposition to tyranny and oppression. And then there is the South's national anthem — *Dixie*.

The South offers an alternative American model, one which is needed in the modern world. The South is the antithesis to modern global hegemony and collectivism. The South is about nationalism, independence, autonomy, personal liberty, limited government. The South embraces God as the sole supreme authority. The South provides an alternative course, alternative direction, an alternative to human secularism and socialism. The South is right.

The old South's conservative ideology important to 2012 election

Democrats and liberals are doing everything they can to divide the South, infiltrating their heritage organizations and dividing conservatives

Will you be manipulated to support Barack Obama indirectly? Will the Libertarians offer you enough reasons to vote for some other candidate who cannot win, or sit out the election. Will you be part of the apathy that will re-elect President Obama? Romney, a Yankee from a deep blue state is your alternative. His heritage and politics are certainly not Southern. So, the liberals who have infiltrated the SCV and other Southern heritage, or political organizations will attempt to distract your political participation in the presidential election away from Romney. There may be a third party candidate similar to Ross Perot ... someone to distract conservatives-libertarians. He or she could never win, but taking your vote from Romney is the target. Will it work?

Romney will say and do enough to make you mad. Even worse than John McCain in some respects, Mitt Romney is not even in your top ten choices for president.

However, Romney did something that you should consider. Mitt Romney went to the NAACP annual meeting and told them he would repeal Obama Care. He said it that specifically and was booed. He did not retreat; he did not apologize. He just said Obama Care has to go. Traditionally, in excess of 90 percent of the black vote goes for the Democrat. Something you should consider when you vote.

We all know that Obama Care is the largest socialist legislation since FDR's Social Security program, the one going bankrupt right now.

These programs are directly contrary to the Confederate Constitution and states' rights. Social Security began the liberal offensive to make people dependent on government. That dependency has taken your liberty. It has placed our very freedoms in jeopardy.

It will take a massive Republican win, not just in the White House, but in both houses of Congress to repeal Obama Care and reverse the massive federal spending burying the nation in debt. Never before has the Southern approach to government, as articulated in the Confederate Constitution been so important.

For the first time in a long time, the Old South and its view concerning national government is very important. The Confederate Constitution addressed many of the problems and issues we face today including: inviting God to the governing table, prohibiting private sector bailouts, reducing the power of the Supreme Court in relation to the states, bringing fiscal responsibility to the national capital through the power of the presidency and the line-item veto.

The South had the vision to see the problems we would face today. Southern patriots created a Constitution which would have prevented the problems we face today. This election gives you a chance to re-assert Southern leadership in national affairs. A united South cannot only secure the White House but can help win enough seats in the US Senate to repeal Obama Care. So what will you do?

The establishment of the SECESSION CLOCK, set at 6 PM

During the Cold War a "Doomsday Clock" was created; today we start a new clock to evaluate how close the US is to seeing a state secede!

During the Cold War, the Doomsday Clock was created as a subjective measure of the possibility of a nuclear exchange between the United States and the Soviet Union. This clock was reset annually when those responsible for evaluating the tensions between the two superpowers and the political environment of the planet made a determination where to set the clock. If memory serves the clock always was in a position between eleven and twelve, usually between ten minutes until midnight and minutes or seconds before midnight.

The Doomsday Clock was used by different special interests as a tool to make the general public and the mainstream media more or less concerned with the possibility of nuclear war. The Doomsday Clock has faded in its importance and visibility to the general public as a result of the victory of the United States over the Soviet Union on Christmas Day 1991. With the end of the Cold War, the Soviet Union collapsed. Some republics held within the Soviet Union seceded and established their own nations! On the world stage, the Soviet Union was replaced by Russia and a *partnership* between the United States and Russia was fabricated. As time has passed, the *partnership* has shown signs of dormancy and the differences between the two nations.

Today, as a result of the most recent decisions of the Supreme Court of the United States, which clearly repudiate the original Constitution of the United States, and thus are placing the reasons for union between the states in jeopardy, I would like to announce through the Nolan Chart that the Confederate War College is establishing, as of this date, the Secession Clock. The purpose of the Secession Clock will be to attempt to evaluate the possibility of secession of one or more states from the Union.

The original position of the Secession Clock on its first day, June 28, 2012, is placed at six o'clock. This original position is selected to demonstrate that secession is now a legitimate point of discussion concerning the future of the United States of America. Since the issue of secession has been a non-starter since Appomattox, the significance of reintroducing the idea of secession as a fundamental American's recourse to a government which is not acting in conformance with the concepts of "the consent of the governed," "rule of the majority," "separation of powers" and the "rule of law."

The Secession Clock is being established because of the decisions of the Supreme Court concerning Obama Care, the decision against the ability of Arizona law enforcement to protect the state from invasion by illegal immigrants (due to the failure of the federal government, under both Republican and Democratic administrations to defend the national border and enforce enacted laws concerning immigration). In addition, the Secession Clock has been created in response to the ongoing process for implementing the United Nations Agenda 21 which does usurp the sovereignty of the United States of America.

On a periodic basis (yet to be established), the Secession Clock will be reset to help the general public of the United States understand both the need for consideration of secession as a legitimate response to the actions of the federal government, and or predict the likelihood of secession by a legal political subdivision of the United States.

While the chancellor of the Confederate War College will make the ultimate decision as to the time to be set on the clock, accepted members of the Confederate War College and other invited persons (all designated as the timekeepers) will be consulted and allowed to place in consideration written statements intended to influence the setting of the time.

A Secession Clock will be created on the homepage of the Confederate War College so the general public from time-to-time can visit the page to review the setting of the Secession Clock.

Why Confederates are taken for granted!

The Confederates of the Southern movement are like the conservatives of the Republican Party ... the leaders believe they have no choice!

The parallels occurring in America between the 2012 election year, what is occurring in America as a nation and in the South, and the events of 150 years ago are startling. While most Americans have some knowledge of the GOP primary, few have any idea of the Sesquicentennial (the 150th Anniversary of the Civil War) and the events occurring in the Southern movement. And yet, what is occurring is like mirror reflections of one another.

Let's start with what most people know about, the GOP primary. Mitt Romney is the sweetheart of the northeast Republicans. He is super rich, someone keenly involved in the international economy. He is a social liberal, the father of Romney Care, the prototype of Obama Care. He is not Christian, or at least his faith, Mormonism, is not Christian, and this suits the northeast elite who revile the Christian faith. God has no place at the governing table. Heavily Catholic in the northeast, it is also heavily liberal. Abortion starts and ends there, along with feminism.

There is a strong Jewish constituency in the northeast, and though divided on many issues, many Jews see America as an extension of Israel, not the other way around ... American foreign policy revolves around Israel. We are in two wars, and threatening a third for Israel's security, not our own.

Former governor of a blue, dark blue state, Mitt Romney is keenly aware of all the above.

But Romney can't win a majority of Republican votes anywhere. He has spent maybe twenty million dollars and the best he can do is garner about 35 per cent of the vote in any state. Why? Because the conservative core of the party rejects him. It's instinctual. It's not Rush or Hannity. They have no effect on this. Neither does Beck, a Mormon, who I would bet is committed to Romney. Beck has backed away recently, but his fangs have already shown.

So if the conservative base will not support Romney in the primaries, how is it the GOP elite think Romney can beat Obama? (Maybe they don't, but that's for a different article.) The Republican elite, the Neo-Cons, the Karl Roves, the Bushes, et.al figure the conservatives have nowhere else to go. If Romney is the nominee, if he is forced on the party, they will have no choice but support him. Some conservatives may stay home, but the Republican elite just can't believe enough of the conservative base would stay home, or vote for Obama to give the Democrats the win. So conservatives ... once again, as you have time and again, you will have to accept the lesser of two evils. You know, like McCain and Bob Dole, this is the best we can do. Suck it up! (an old Army expression)

For most of us conservatives we know the story. It's burned in our political memories.

Well, the parallel is in the South. For most of the nation the Sesquicentennial doesn't mean much. Many Americans' ancestors arrived after the war. Italians, central Europeans, Greeks, and almost all the Latinos have no direct connection to the war or the division of the nation. In fact, most of these people have no connection to the founding of the nation. They came for material wealth, not liberty and freedom. In their mind, government is supposed to provide. The Tenth Amendment, what's that?

But in the South, where there is a tie to Robert E. Lee, the Confederacy, and Southern nationalism, the Sesquicentennial is more than a minor occurrence. If you have ever seen the movie *Sweet Home Alabama*, it accurately portrays what occurs in the South every year! The Sesquicentennial is *NOT* the only time reenactments occur — it's just when the biggest ones do. A special effort is made.

Recent work at Texas A&M on genealogical formulas indicates between 50 and 80 million Americans have blood that traces back to a Southern ancestor — that would be one sixth to one fourth of all Americans. A pretty sizeable crew.

But the Sesquicentennial is occurring during the Obama presidency and there seems to be a real effort, though hidden and underground, to reduce the Southern pride. Example: the Museum of the Confederacy (MOC) Located in the heart of Richmond, the capitol of the old Confederacy, the museum occupies prized ground which surrounding hospitals or other businesses want. The pressure has been on them a long time to get out. So, this year, the MOC opens its first extension. Many of us believe the opening of such extensions will allow the museum to leave Richmond eventually.

But the selection for the first opening is evidence that Yankee interests have invested the museum.

Is the first opening in the lovely Shenandoah where Jackson beat three Union armies in one campaign? No. Oh, I know, it's off Interstate 95 at Chancellorsville, the site of Lee's greatest victory! No. OK, maybe up closer to Washington, DC, on the Manassas battlefield where the Confederacy won two major battles? Nope. So where?

Appomattox, the place where General Lee surrendered the Army of Northern Virginia. You are kidding! For a Southerner only Andersonville could be a worse location!

Nope, it's Appomattox. A location more than an hour away from any interstate! A location not heavily visited. Great plan, don't you think? Take the museum out of Richmond and put it out in the middle of nowhere?

But the subtle attack on the Confederacy gets better. No Confederate Flags will fly on poles outside the Museum of the Confederacy! Not one.

But hey, you Southerners dig into your pockets and shell out some money for the MOC

The fight in the South goes well beyond this.

At The Citadel in Charleston, South Carolina, where the cadets of this school fired the first shots of the war, this school played *Dixie* as its fight song at football games in the '70s. Confederate naval ensigns flew proudly on the RVs and cars outside the stadium at the cookouts before the game. Crimson red dominated the area surrounding the stadium

Crimson red still dominates, but it's not the Confederate Battle Flag. And *Dixie*, well you don't hear that one anymore. The Citadel is not the only culprit. The University of Texas at Arlington, which used to be Arlington State College, and was known as the Rebels where *Dixie* was also played, is now the UTA Mavericks. The effort to erase Southern history proceeds unabated. The heritage organizations responsible for defending the *Cause*, overwhelmed or apathetic, shrink in inactivity. Oh yes, every once in awhile you will hear about a court case. But with a potential base of 50-80 million Americans, you would think they could make more than a whisper.

Where Gettysburg in Pennsylvania, nets three hundred million in tourist monies every year, employing 6,000 people, battlefields in the South are hidden. When you drive into a Southern state, go to their visitor's center and look through the brochures for maps about the Civil War. Probably won't find them. They are there but you have to ask at the counter. The North can prosper from the war, but the South … nope.

Groups like the Sons of Confederate Veterans and the United Daughters of the Confederacy treat Southern patriots like the GOP treats their conservative core. You have nowhere else to go, so suck it up!

OK, so why are you writing this article? Well, Republicans, remember you thought the conservatives would have no choice? If there is a parallel between the South and the GOP, you better rethink that.

In the South, since the heritage organizations would not fight for the South, new groups have spontaneously arisen, and you know what? Much of the activists in these groups are members of the heritage organizations who are tired of inactivity and defeat without a fight. They are in the streets, and they call themselves Flaggers. They reject the passivity and leadership of the heritage organizations. They are causing more pressure on the enemies of the South, and getting more attention than anyone can believe. They are only a handful, but in a South tired of being kicked, they are growing.

Well, the same could happen in November at the ballot box.

Sarah Palin is still with us. A candidacy by her would end Romney, nominee or not.

History does repeat itself … but this time the history is simultaneous. Patriotism is not dead. Individuals willing to fight for what they think is right, and who are tired of sorry leadership, are on the move. Will it snowball? Let's watch.

Southern media spin about Dixie hurts the South!

The South is still enduring reconstruction; Southern news media's PC reporting is detrimental to its viewers!

Recently, reports about a new "Flags Across the South" project in Paducah, KY, received a less than favorable report by local television station WPSD-TV.

Are reporters at Southern stations naive, or are they knowingly repeating scare tactics and false representations of the Confederate Battle Flag to divide the South and repress Southern patriotism? Do they know the history of the South, and of the Sons of Confederate Veterans? And do they know the Confederate Battle Flag is the most recognized symbol of the South in the entire world? Have they ever realized the South is the only region in the United States with a symbol and quasi-national anthem!

Do they know people across the world use the South's colors when acting against repressive, tyrannical, occupying governments? (See the Berlin Wall and Afghanistan to start with.) When is the last time any Southern media did a serious report on the Confederate Flag or the heritage organizations like the SCV and UDC?

Do they know that heritage organizations annually condemn racist groups for misuse of the Confederate colors? I wonder if those reporters even know it is the Sesquicentennial (150th Anniversary) of the late unpleasantness?

These questions lead to even other questions. Do Southern television stations intentionally hire from outside the South? Are they in cahoots with the other media to make a vanilla America, stripped of her regional identities? Is there an intentional plan to homogenize America?

The media are not the only Southerners delinquent in their love of the South. The Southern heritage organizations do a pitiful job of media relations. There is no national or state plans to encourage and help local camps to visit their local media, TV, radio, and print and familiarize them with the Sons of Confederate Veterans, United Daughters of the Confederacy, the history of the South, and the importance of knowing the Rebel flag is an internationally known and revered symbol of the South.

Men like the leaders of the Sons of Confederate Veterans are really good men whose hearts are dedicated to the *Cause*. Just this past weekend, in Jasper, Alabama, a local group of the SCV, the Hutto Camp, held ceremonies to honor the Confederate Memorial in the town square. A copy of the remarks (titled Confederate Memorial Day and its relevance today) is available at the Confederate War College.

Unfortunately, there are just too many in the SCV organization which obstruct real efforts to grow the organization, and most importantly, vindicate the Cause.

To illustrate just how weak the SCV is in media work, when the Texas Division press

With Grits and All The Fixins — 11

person was asked to circulate a statewide press release, he replied he did not have a statewide media contact list! Now the media person in Texas is a good man and has held that position for a number of years, but because the failure of the Texas leadership to use him resulted in a press person without a statewide list. The grannies in Texas just sleep. (Not all in Texas are grannies, just the leadership, including most of the state board, known as the DEC.)

In any event, a statewide media contact list was generated in less than a day! And the release went out. (If there are states who have plans handed down to their camps to approach local media, please annotate that at the end of this article so other states may benefit from your work.) Compatriots (members of the SCV) and their sisters in the UDC across the South work hard to do what they can to vindicate the *Cause*. But a lot of the leadership of these organizations are just not up to the real work and confrontation required.

When you consider there are between 50-80 million living descendants of Confederate veterans in America today, you would think Southern heritage organizations would be booming. Activist organizations are springing up all over the South because the heritage organizations just are not combat effective in the Culture War. (See those organizations in other columns in *America Today*.)

But back to the main point of the article. It's time for Southerners to realize you live in the South — that the South is a great place to live. Southerners should be proud the trends demonstrate a mass migration from the northeast and mid-west to the South. And, that the Southern battle flag and *Dixie* are priceless trademarks of the South. It's time to get them out of the closet, polish them up, and re-educate both the northern immigrants and many born in here in the South to the honors and values of the Southern symbols and Southern people. And there are black spokespersons, like H. K. Edgerton, who have spent decades of their lives telling the story of the South. They should be a big part of this regional renovation work.

It's time to get the Southern media on the side of Dixie! And if there are any Southern media who want to take this up, I would be more than willing to help you with an interview. Contact me at johnyreb43@yahoo.com.

Send your comments concerning the WPSD coverage to WPSD-TV 100 Television Lane Paducah, KY 42003 Main 270-415-1900 Fax - 270-415-1981 Newsroom 270-415-2001 and encourage them to get up to date on the South!

Christmas on Rebel Mountain, Texas

A noise outside led to one heck of a discovery!

A Rebel Mountain Story of Christmas I'm fixing to tell you is something interesting, which you are never gonna' believe.

Grab a hot cup of cider and settle down in your chair. Christmas Eve night was kind of cold and drizzly. I woke up sometime after midnight 'cause I heard something outside. There's been lots of coyotes round, and we just had a brood of baby goats … kids. So I got up, put on my Citadel-blue bathrobe, grabbed my .35 caliber lever-action rifle and headed out the backdoor towards the pasture.

It was dark; heavy clouds obstructed the Milky Way. I didn't turn on any lights 'cause all they do is ruin my night vision. I heard the light clamor of bells, the clinks getting louder as I walked out the hundred yards towards my pasture. At first I thought I saw a really large eight-point buck, then another right behind the first … then a couple more, all standing in line, harnessed. And behind the deer was a huge red sleigh.

In the front seat of the sleigh was a furry red jacket, with white trim and a red Santa hat. The back of the sleigh was almost empty … a lot of empty brown canvas bags, a few still containing wrapped presents. As I turned the back corner of the sleigh, there he was. He had a full head of white bushy hair and beard. His boots were a polished, shiny black, his pants red, but his shirt, was kind of gray and woolly. And he had a gray kepi on his head! In his hand he had a small bottle of what appeared to be milk. He was slightly bent over and was feeding Noah … one of the kids, a baby goat whose mother had rejected him at birth so we are bottle feeding. How Santa knew that, I will never know. But little Noah's tail was busy wagging, and you could hear the sucking sound on the bottle.

Well, I lowered my rifle and walked on towards Santa. Last time I had seen evidence of him, I was seven. His footprints were in the snow from our chimney to our neighbor's chimney. I had never seen him, but those footprints sure were solid evidence to me at the time. Santa, turned his head as heard me approaching,

"Evening," he said, "Noah is getting a special treat tonight." Santa chuckled.

I paused only a moment; I had no trouble with accepting this was Santa. I walked up close to him, setting my rifle on its butt with its barrel resting against a fence post. I wanted to visit with him. And he was obliging, so we talked some.

"Could I make some coffee inside for ya?" I asked.

"No, I really can't stay that long," he said.

"Yes, I guess you have a lot more homes to do."

"Not really, I am fixin' to finish up," he said with a Southern drawl, "I always end my night in Dixie; I was born in the South, you know."

"Really," I said, "Where were you born?" He looked at me as if I should know, "Have you ever heard of the music group, Alabama?" "Yes, they are my favorite, and I have two of their Christmas albums!" I said proudly.

"Well, I was born just down the road from where they were born in the mountains in northeast Alabama! Why do you think I wear so much red? I thought everyone knew," as he turned his attention back to little Noah who was sucking mostly air, as the bottle was just about empty.

"I didn't know that," I said, "So I guess flying north to go home may not be your favorite part of the night?"

He handed me the bottle and walked around the back of the sleigh up to the front where his jacket and hat were on the seat. He put them on, climbed back in the sleigh and looked down at me with a smile. "That stuff about the North Pole is some more of the revisionist Yankee history," he said with a twinkle in his eye.

My face kind of crinkled up, and I asked "How's that?"

"Mrs. Claus and I and the elves live at the South Pole!" He chuckled as his whip cracked sharply in the night sky. The deer seemed to come to attention, and with the second crack the sleigh began to move, to pull forward, and in just a couple of yards, the lead deer were in the air. The sleigh followed quietly, lifting into the air. I had not noticed 'til that moment, but as the sleigh pulled away and rose in to the sky, I saw a Crimson battle flag spread, waving and snapping, its pole anchored in the right rear corner of the sleigh,

The last words I heard him say in his deep booming voice, against the jingle of the bells on his deer's harness, was "Merry Christmas, Southland …."

A Yankee I would listen to — Jed Marum

Of no import whatsoever, unless peace of mind is what you seek.

Every once in a while God places a gift on the path before you. It's totally unexpected, and there seems no rhyme or reason for it. One second it's a regular day, nothing special. In fact, when you come upon the gift, it may not seem like much at all. I mean it's something nice, but nothing you immediately understand as a special gift. That happened to me when I went to a Confederate living history event down in the area of Houston and ran up on an entertainer. His name is Jed Marum.

Jed is a Yankee, born and raised in Massachusetts, and is of Irish descent. Some of his kin came across from Ireland during the war.

Jed has a gift. He can tell stories through music. He has a good voice, and plays a good guitar. And he writes music. But why Jed was a special gift to me is because he has a real curiosity about the South. Jed does not pretend to be Southern. In fact, one of his songs is titled, "I Didn't Know I was a Yankee 'til I Moved to Texas."

Jed has an advantage. He sees the South as someone foreign. And so what he sees is without the natural bias of Southern blood. But what he sees is the South that is real; he sees the goodness of the South, the Irish-Scot heritage of the South.

Jed has a unique approach in some of his music. He attempts to tell the story of the American war from the Southern perspective. And he takes on events or issues which are not politically correct. For example, one song he wrote tells the story of a Confederate coming home to a war-ravaged Missouri. In another song, Jed talks about the terrorist, John Brown, from the Southern view. His music has a point — one not often told. And it's written in a modern, casual easy-listening style which soothes and gets your toe tapping.

A couple of months after I met Jed, the two of us were featured at a Fort Worth Sons of Confederate Veterans Camp Christmas gathering. Jed provided the music, and I was honored to give the evening's comments. It was scary to have to follow Jed. He is really talented and you could listen to him all night. I kind of felt like I was interrupting his performance when I got up to speak. Maybe it helped keep my comments brief, so that we could get Jed back up.

If you are Southern and you have an event coming up, whether it be something to do with history or something personal like a wedding or graduation, or you just are bringing some friends together for something special, I highly recommend Jed Marum (www.jedmarum.com). He is worth the money. And if you are Irish, well, that's even more of a reason to reach out to Jed.

No, we are not partners. Hell, I would be surprised if Jed even remembers me. But for me, the regionalism of America was a very special part of the America in which I was born. That regionalism is being homogenized and America is losing a very important part of itself. Jed's work takes us back to those days — the days when America represented a kind of Christian united nations. Call Jed and reach back to a City on the Hill, to the glades of Erin, to the dream that was America.

Cross over the River, a Confederate Collection wins Album of the Year

Not your normal subject matter, but Jed Marum composer, picker and singer created an album which trumped all telling the story of the South!

Every year tens of thousands, if not hundreds of thousands of Southerners participate in parades, battle reenactments, cotillions, balls and living history to portray and celebrate the South and its past. The interest in the South is much larger than those who take time to relive and recreate the noble and tragic history of Dixie. The South is alive today. No, not a South which embraces slavery, but a South that embraces Christ, the Southland and all its mysteries and magic. The South is not dead, rather a revival of its culture, pride, and unique regional identity is percolating just below the surface. No, a visiting Yankee might not see it. But if you turn off the paved road and get back where the creek runs through the woods, well you might not only find a still brewing *white lightening*, but maybe you may even hear a tune floating through the air. Follow that tune.

You see there is a man, Jed Marum, who is singing in taverns and inns, at crossroads and meetings. Boston born, Jed is Celt, and his roots are deep. When he moved from the northeast to Texas some years ago, it was as if his soul had found its home. One of his most humorous tunes is *I didn't know I was Yankee 'til I moved to Texas*. Few songs I have heard so truly tell of the unique character and traits of Texas in the brevity and wit of this foot stomping tune.

Jed be blessed with one of the truest of Irish gifts, he can tell a yarn with not only words, but song.

Jed is storyteller, a musician, a composer who is gifted in his ability to conjure up, and express in ballads the feelings of the Celts of the South one hundred and fifty years ago. He is comfortable with the logic and soul which originally brought us the melodies of Scotland and Ireland. He is so comfortable that he writes modern music which brings forth the spirit of the Celts who were the heart of gray-clad legions defending the South from an invading horde intent on conquering and breaking the spirit of Dixie.

But, there are a lot of men across the South who can pick a guitar, or banjo, and harmonize the great songs of the past. But there are not too many who can write modern-day memories of the past. In 2009 Jed's melodies and lyrics in *Cross Over the River, A Confederate Collection* earned JP Folk Album Of The Year!

The story of the South is not often told, and very little known even by people who are born in Dixie today. For example, how do you think a Southerner would have felt about the hanging of the terrorist John Brown? Do today's students or citizens realize the very first man killed at Harper's Ferry, Virginia, by John Brown was a free black man?! Or, what thoughts went through the minds of the men who rode to Lawrence, Kansas, to repay a vengeful debt for Yankee atrocities against Southerners in Missouri?

And then there's *Shenandoah's* run, a musical tale which tells of the final days of the Confederacy's last commerce raider. The *Shenandoah* operated in the northern Pacific and Bering Sea obliterating the Yankee whaling fleet of the day! When its captain learned of the surrender of the Confederacy a decision had to be made, what to do with the noble *Shenandoah*? Listen to this song and find out!

And if your blood fought in the bloody battles of the western theatre, whether you be rooted in Yankeeland or the magnolias of the South, you know of the South's most famous Irish general, Patrick Cleburne. Jed's ballad, titled *Stonewall of the West*, fills an Irishman with the pride we feel when we remember our great warriors.

There are old traditional songs like *Cindy, Shenandoah,* and *Backland Races*. And still other songs of Jed's composition; *Come Back Katy, Monaghan's Lament, Hard Times* and *After the Dance*. Simply put, this is an album I can't stop playing.

But when I do, I reach for another of Jed's. Jed's music reaches past the American Civil War to tell the story of the Celts over centuries. My favorite is *Sands of Aberdeen*. These collections of songs demonstrate the softer side of Jed, and bring peace to my being. As the world, through *diversity* moves to homogeneity I long for my own past, my own traditions and loves. You see I am Irish, Scot, German and Southern. For me, I could ask for no more in terms of the past that has been mixed in my blood. Jed touches three of those lines in a way only a descendant can feel.

Jed's music is available at his site. But to be honest, to really enjoy him, you need to bring him to you. Jed travels nationwide. Contact him, see what you can work out. The larger your event, the more you will be very happy you were able to bring him to your people. But don't be afraid to contact him for anything, small or large. I sit with a smile on my face … I know Jed and believe I can call him a "kin soul."

As You Were! Citadel Cadet Stories from The Past, by Ted Childress

Funny, descriptive, this brief concoction of Citadel life is a good read.

Charleston, South Carolina and The Citadel are in many ways the symbolic heart of the land known as Dixie. It was here in Charleston that the cadets of The Citadel fired the first shots against Yankee oppression when the USS *Star of the West* was sent by President Buchanan to reinforce and resupply Ft. Sumter in January, 1861. The culture, history, architecture, food and beauty of her women make Charleston a place every Southerner should visit. And The Citadel, the top ranked public college in the South, is a place where citizen-soldier leaders have been molded since 1842!

Whether you are an alumnus of The Citadel, a present-day cadet, or someone totally unfamiliar with the joys and unique experience of Spartan life, you will really enjoy this well written, humorous book. Ted Childress did an excellent job of painting the picture of cadet life in Charleston a half a century ago. I had the pleasure of meeting Ted in the bookstore at The Citadel during the 2012 Homecoming weekend. Ted is a graduate of the South's bastion for patriotism, a former Army infantry officer and a retired academic. But, I believe Ted's real talent may be in storytelling.

As we often do, my wife read a book aloud as we travelled the roads necessary to return home to East Texas from the South's premier coastal city. I had not been back to Charleston in 15 years, and it looks good! I mean really good. Money has been invested there. Old neighborhoods have not been bulldozed down. Instead, the old homes have been renovated and repaired. They look like a newer, cleaner, brighter version of the very same dingy, sad homes I remember walking past a score, a decade and five years ago! Great work Charleston!

Dr. Childress' book is really a good read. Filled with a number of true stories, which might qualify as legends for the Corps, this magnificent work brings back memories, but also demonstrates how much the Corps has retained the traditions, discipline, comradeship and mischievous side of those who wear the Citadel ring. Though I went to Citadel a good fifteen years after Ted, I found very few things had changed from his time to mine. His Corps was imaginative in their pranks, but my gut tells me a few hours downing some beers with my classmates would bring back to our joint conscience equally ingenious shenanigans!

I don't want to spoil his stories, so I won't go in to any details here. However, to whet your appetite I shall briefly mention some of the more important characters, places and topics of this excellent bundle of tales. Maybe the most startling to me were his recollections of one of America's most renown military figures, Dwight D. Eisenhower. I never knew this man of mythic proportions visited The Citadel campus, not once, but twice. When you read the story of this great American visiting the Corps, you will get a glimpse of how one man can affect so many with one decision! Not to be outdone, President John F. Kennedy visited the Corps, but his visit had a different impact … read the book!

One very important part of book for me, was his reminding me of the importance of General Mark Wayne Clark. Commander of the US Armed Forces in Italy during World War II. General Clark served as president of The Citadel in the years following the war. His contributions to the Corps, and the reputation of The Citadel may never be truly known by those of us who enjoy the benefits he brought to our school.

Ted's stories about the Corps mess hall are funny, though his remembrances of the food served and mine are quite different. Yes, we both had *mystery meat*. Ted didn't like it, I did. He didn't mention the term "waitee," a term of endearment we used in my time in the Corps for the women who served our food. I am curious as to whether his Corps used it? Or does today's Corps use it?

Maybe the most telling of his stories is his first. Do you know what "hairy socks" are? I didn't until I read his story. It is a great opening story because it illustrates just how far a freshman cadet will go to overcome a challenge.

I strongly recommend Dr. Childress' book to you. If you are in any way connected to The Citadel, or if you lived in a military environment this work may ignite memories. If you have not had that experience, this book will give you a brief glimpse at a life very strange, very isolated, but which has been highly successful in developing the character and potential of those who can survive it.

Confederate War College moves Secession Clock up one hour!

A variety factors within, and without, of America indicate the political environment for secession is percolating in the United States.

The Confederate War College (CWC) announces the committee responsible for the setting of the Secession Clock has decided, by split decision, to move the clock forward a full hour to 7 PM. The committee took weeks to consider the question and advanced the clock which attempts to reflect the mood of the American people towards the idea of secession.

The committee offers the following reasons — observations for the advancement of the clock. Moving the clock forward by one hour translates to 16 percent of the available time between 6 PM and 12 o'clock. This is a large move forward, but one the CWC feels is justifiable because:

a. Secession has been a topic of discussion on national conservative radio talk shows like Sean Hannity and Glen Beck. Though both talk show hosts dismissed the idea of secession, the very fact the topic was even discussed demonstrates its rising viability in the minds of the American people.

b. Recently, secession has been a topic of articles written by nationally syndicated writers like Pat Buchanan and Walter Williams.

c. A recent *Huffington Post* poll found 22 percent of Americans support the idea of their state seceding from the union. An extraordinarily large number considering there has been relatively little public discussion of this issue until very recently.

d. All fifty states have had committees within the state file petitions for secession.

e. A Constitutional crisis maybe pending concerning Obama Care and its implementation. A number of states have passed nullification legislation concerning their participation in Obama Care. The *Washington Times* recently ran an article about jury nullification of Obama Care. Twenty-one states have refused to establish the insurance exchanges required in President Obama's health care legislation. All of this occurring as Washington looks over the Fiscal Cliff.

f. Governor Rick Perry of Texas has spoken of secession publicly, and while he has wavered on this issue, it has drawn national attention. Liberals like Rivera way overreacted to even the mention of secession. The liberals are scared to death because this is really the only check on federal power, and the very mention of secession questions the principle of "consent of the governed" in the United States of America. If we start openly talking about secession, then they have to deal with that!

g. Secession is not a US alternative only. Scotland is set to vote in national referendum in 2014 on leaving the United Kingdom! Other nations or peoples around the world are also looking at independence.

The issue of secession is a very sensitive one. Liberals react violently to any mention of this political alternative, point to the American Civil War as resolving the issue, and almost always attach slavery to the issue of secession to demean its legitimacy. But conservatives and others see secession as the only real check on the massing power of the central government and the destruction of the republican form of government. While secession has traditionally been associated with the South, the modern secession movement is active throughout the United States and not unique to one region or the other.

"The Confederate War College does not have a position concerning secession at this time, though it does defend the Constitutional right of the sovereign states which formed the United States to divorce as was originally intended when the Constitution was approved by the respective states."

The Confederate War College maintains the Secession Clock as a simple means to reflect the mood of the American people and provide a point of discussion for the concept of secession as a peaceful political alternative to today's constant disputes between an expanding central government and the states and people.

Do Southern Democrats embrace their party's rejection of God?

It's the exception within a big tent Democratic Party, Christianity has been rejected by Obama, by the party, will you vote for that?

The platform of a political party is intended to express the general consensus of the party with respect to their philosophy to address issues and challenges to our nation, The platform is intended to prescribe solutions and initiatives for the government to manifest; and to express the purpose of our country. While it is not a binding compulsory statement or litmus test for individual members or representatives, it is supposed to represent a broad consensus of view within a party.

So when Democrats removed God from their platform and then had a vicious floor fight to re-invite God back into the party, it was not just a political detail for political junkies.

Rejecting God is not new for the Democrats. For example, the Democrats refuse Pro Life speakers at their conventions. Despite the slaughter of fifty million innocent unborn souls in America, many of those deaths in one of the Democratic Party's foundational constituencies, the African-Americans, the Democratic Party does not allow public discussion of the practice of abortion. Genocide appears to be an accepted policy within the Democratic Party.

A second foundational constituency within the Democratic Party is much of the membership of the Roman Catholic Church. The Catholic faith opposes abortion articulating the belief that murder of the unborn is a sin. And yet, Pro Life speakers are barred from the Democratic Party. Censorship is strictly imposed. A caste system within the Democratic Party places the wants and desires of one caste, women, above another caste, the unborn. And the Catholics, whether they be citizens or leaders, Priests or just members of the Church are discouraged from addressing this "right to life" issue at the Democrat Convention.

Before I go further, ask yourself; Do I want to belong to, or vote for, a party that has the audacity to believe it has the right to take life, and further has the right to censor its membership? Is that the kind of people I want to associate with? Whether I believe in God or not, do I believe I have the right silence others who do not agree with me? Do I have the right to take another's life?

And ask yourself, do you trust man to be good enough to set the limits of right and wrong? Do you have faith a majority will always be right? Do you trust your life to the whim of the majority? Do you believe right and wrong is constantly in flux? Is something wrong today, right tomorrow? And if something right today, is wrong tomorrow, do you accept the punishment for doing wrong when it was right?

I know there are a lot of mental somersaults here. But, when the Democrats in Convention took God out of their platform, and then when an attempt was made to invite God back into the Democratic Party's the effort received loud and continuous boos. Can you imagine booing God? Does this mean it was Democrats who called Barabbas and called for Jesus to be crucified? Is that the group of people you want to belong to?

These are not the only examples of atheism and agnosticism in the Democratic Party. President Obama himself publicly declared America is not a Christian nation. Seventy-eight percent of Americans identify themselves as Christian, but we are not Christian? The very men who founded this nation over and over again pointed to Christianity and God at the founding of the nation. Our national character, and our national definitions of right and wrong come from the Bible. Yet, President Obama denies we are a Christian nation. Is this the party you want to be your representative?

And of course there was the Obama attack on the Catholic Church, attempting to force the Church to pay for abortions and birth control for their employees. Separation of Church and State sure didn't mean too much when the Obama Administration attempted to force the Church to comply with the rules of the state!

In the South, Christianity still permeates most aspects of life. The Bible Belt as it is known, used to be a geographical anchor of the Democrat Party. Three of the South's states, Florida, North Carolina and Virginia were states Obama won in the 2008 election. Will these states, one of them the home of the Reverend Billy Graham, accept and embrace the "boos" of the Charlotte Convention!? Will these Southern states reject God?

And another constituency which many political pundits believe are the future of America, the Hispanics, will they accept the rabid attacks against their Church, and God? Will Hispanics place immigration, or welfare checks above their faith? Will Hispanics, with their votes, accept the superiority of the state over the Church?

Certainly the economy is an important issue in 2012. Romney-Ryan does provide an alternative to the failed Obama policies. US energy independence by 2020 would be the catalyst and lubricant for a rebuilt American economic engine! But more than that, there is a spiritual aspect to the Republican campaign, one built on the personal religious faith of Romney and Ryan.

Could a massive shift in the Hispanic vote, based on their religious belief realign them to the political right, and in so doing create the political firmament for some kind of immigration compromise? Would conservatives, especially social conservatives see the new alignment as something good for America?

American has been shifting right on the issue of abortion for years. Could an Hispanic realignment with the GOP finally push this issue to critical mass?

No one can down play, or claim the Democratic Party merely made a bureaucratic mistake at their convention in Charlotte. The evidence of their continuous rejection of God may be best illustrated by "the boos" at the Democrat Convention, but those boos are only the verbal evidence of a long trail of secularism.

Let's outline a new national second political party called Dixiecrat!

The Democrats have an identity and agenda, the Republicans do not. A new party is needed to offer a modern American alternative view!

Destruction or abandonment of the Republican Party and the formation of a new national second party is the best hope for turning America's course towards prosperity and security. The ongoing battle within the Republican Party clearly shows the majority of the people within the GOP are dissatisfied with the RINO-ruling elite Republican Party which does not offer a true alternative to the socialism and human secularism of the Democratic Party. Most Republicans would agree at the national level the Republican Party is Democrat-Lite and that simply is not a real alternative. The social liberal-fiscal conservatives of the northeast who pretend to be Republicans are really just hand-me-downs from the Democrats. They offer nothing in terms of a second choice. But for better or worse, this RINO Republicanism is evident in most Senators, including Marco Rubio, Graham of South Carolina, and others.

So America desperately needs a new national party. This new party must offer a real vision for the future based on how the world is now, and the realities of new technologies and the fluid nature of the technological explosion that is the new frontier in human relations.

This new party must be based on a realistic comprehensive survey of the modern world that identifies;

a the growing ambitions of both nation-states like the People's Republic of China, combined with the arrival of nations like Brazil, India, Pakistan and others on to the world stage, and

b. an understanding that Islam is the faith of one quarter of the world's population, spread through a number of nations, and that religious faith is a real and permanent component of human development and

c the evolution of a new global class, representing international corporations and an intelligentsia intent on world governance and elimination of the nation-state control much the media the American people see each day. And that globalism is the next *ism threat* to the United States.

d. an understanding that by placing America's domestic and economic policy future in the hands of the fifty states we avoid the very dangerous risk of placing all the eggs in one basket in terms of investment, commercial activity, social fashions and threats. Allowing America to be the world's democratic laboratory system protects our nation from central collapse. When uncontrolled chaotic advance occurs across the spectrum of human activity it seems wise to consolidate central power to those things which must be done at the central level, and to delegate as much as possible to the states so that human ingenuity and multiple choices can be implemented.

The survey must talk about where the world is today; whose friends with who, who shares interests with who, and that our security as a nation can be threatened by not only rival nation-states, but uncontrolled immigration, technological development, shortages of food and energy reserves and internal political agendas which seek to end national sovereignty. The survey should also speak to the exhaustion the nation feels as a result of more than half a century as world leader — policeman, and the roles of nations like Japan, and those of Europe doing their fair share to maintain the world economy.

Americans need to know where we are. What is probable in the next half century? Does America have a role in space separate and apart from other nations? Is space one of the next great frontiers? Does space exploration and colonization have a place in our national security planning?

Essential to the conduct of the survey is who does it? Who pays for it? Will we get a survey slanted to someone's agenda, or will get a true bird's eye view of what is now, and will be in the not to distant future?

Then the new party needs a philosophical foundation. The name Dixiecrat is important because it fits the ideology I propose should be at the core of the new party. Let's make it clear from the beginning that as I propose it Dixiecrat is not an exclusively a Southern Party, but rather a party which can see many of the advantages offered through a more confederated nation where the states are the chief policy makers for domestic issues. The fundamental goals for the new party should be;

a. An acknowledgement of Christianity and God as the bedrock of the nation, and the source of right and wrong. This moral and philosophical foundation should be Judeo-Christian in nature, not choosing one church over another, but rather choosing the Bible and God over all. This principle traces its very roots back to Columbus and the discovery of America. The work *The Christian Character* and *Life of the Civil Institutions of the United States* should be one of central scholarly works used to conceptualize the place of God in governance and in caring for the people.

The concept of Christian charity should take the place of government welfare programs for example.

As was the case in the early days of the union, religious faith is a matter of choice for each individual. However, diversity for its own purpose should *NOT* be a guiding principle. The character of the nation is best measured in its individual citizens and thus Christianity must be prevalent and predominant in the people.

It should be clear that and human freedom is a gift, and condition given by God, and it is because of God the political concept of equality of each individual is a worthy foundational concept for the new Republic. Both liberty and political equality were given by God, and thus are core components of the new Constitution.

b. As was the reality when the United States was founded, the state(s) should be recognized as both the creator of the Republic and as the single most important political sub division of the new Republic. The state should be the ultimate the authority concerning domestic social issues. The states should be the source of revenue for the central government. The income tax at the federal level should be abolished, and the IOUs of social security transferred to the states.

An aspect of the republic which has been almost run from existence is regionalism. Yet, it was the regionalism that manifested choice, setting different priorities, preserving unique cultures while creating new ones. Regionalism can work financially to take back the electronic media. There must be multiple voices, multiple American accents, devoid of European influence.

c. Assimilation of migrants to the American way must be at the core of the Dixiecrat Party. The foundational pillars of Christianity — Constitution — national patriotism — capitalism is essential to America 21st Century. And this assimilation must be actual, not academic. Assimilation must happen at the community and state, and cannot be a government affirmative action plan where groups of people become dependent and addicted to government handouts. Instead it must weave the migrants, one at a time, into the commercial, cultural and political activities of day to day life.

Shutting off the free flow of illegal immigration would go a long way towards increasing the value of unskilled labor and skilled labor. It would ignite market forces that to this point have rested dormant because of unlimited unskilled labor — thus allowing for the great divide in terms of income at the bottom, from the top. You don't need a minimum wage if labor, whether it be digging ditches, or laying pipe, or using a hammer is in demand. Unions are an artificial stimulant, much like drugs, which allow for short periods of unreality before reality crashes back in.

The limited role of the Federal government should be reaffirmed through the Constitution. The Tenth Amendment should be the guiding the light for the Supreme Court when deciding competing interests between the states and people, and the central government. State borders should be more than administrative lines on a map, but important boundaries of social policy. Federal monies should be prohibited from being spent on social issues within a state. State law should be supreme in social issues so as to provide the most diversity within the United States. The old, but wise idea of seeing the individual states as laboratories of democracy should rise as a principle of governance.

Through the history of the United States the self-evident roles of the central government have become obvious; National defense, protection/security of the border, foreign relations based on a defense of American national interests are necessary. The creation of national money system, and as the guardian of free trade within the Union are all necessary.

But the term republic has never been more appropriate in terms of manifesting choice and allowing multiple choices to develop as they will so as to offer the best chance for prosperity.

Finally, this avenue of approach or ideology is too contrary to how things exist today, and to present special interests that it cannot be embraced by the existing Republican Party. The existing party simply is not built to allow a new beginning, one focused on Christ and nationalism. The Republican Party is just too *sold out*, too infested with a wide array of special interests to be the mother of a new America resurgent in the oldest foundations of the nation. The new party must begin in the states because it is the states who have the most to gain. Parties must spring up through out America, separately but founded on common American value sets. Then those state parties must fuse together with one of the main common denominators being the primacy of the Tenth Amendment in the new America.

For a true American revival we need a true core of ideological believers … all we need do it look to the liberals to see how to do it. A new party offers a new hope, and a chance to break out of the immoral — secular — no value hedgerows that our nation is currently mired in.

Section II

The Confederate Battle Flag as a Symbol of the South

The Rebel Flag has orbited earth, did you see it?

Why is there so much hatred towards the Confederate battle flag?

Never More Relevant; Never More Important

The Rebel Flag has orbited earth — did you see it?

In 2006, on the International Space station the symbol of America's Southland flew in space!

Most Southerners, most Americans would be shocked to learn that during the War for Southern Independence, 1861-1865, the Confederate Naval ensign, the flag many know as the Rebel flag or the Crimson Cross, actually flew in harbors in South America, Europe, the Caribbean and even the ports of China! The Confederacy's last truly successful commerce raider, the CSS *Shenandoah* actually operated between Alaska and Russia in the Bering Sea, savaging the American whaling fleet in the last months of the war. If you are interested in learning about the Confederate Navy, I suggest to you *Service Afloat* by Admiral Rafael Semmes, CSN, and *The History of the Confederate States Navy* by J. Thomas Scharf, a graduate of the Confederate Naval Academy (yep, they had one) and veteran of the CSN Scharf is the father of Confederate Naval history.

The CSN (Confederate States Navy) was as daring and bold, as ingenious and tenacious as their land counterparts in the Army of Northern Virginia, armies of Tennessee and Mississippi, or the forty-eight Irish Catholic Confederates under the command of Lt. Dick Dowling, who defeated and repulsed a Union invasion armada of more than twenty warships and a five-thousand Yankee infantry at Sabine Pass, Texas, in September 1863. A stunning victory which revived Southern morale after the twin defeats at Gettysburg and Vicksburg.

There is much history covered in dust in the libraries of the United States which might reignite the glory and nobility of the South.

A really obvious example of modern-day revisionism is the fact so few people worldwide, and especially in America, heard the news the Confederate Naval ensign actually orbited the earth in the International Space Station in 2006.

I don't know; I don't watch much mainstream television, so maybe the flying of the Confederate Battle Flag at the International Space Station is old news! Maybe you all have already heard this story told back in 2006 by MSN News.

It seems a Russian astronaut carried ten Confederate Flags to the station where they were photographed, stamped with the seal of the I.S.S., autographed and returned to earth for eventual sale at auction by eBay. Of course, once the left discovered this, the story briefly flared like a sun spot, and the Russian astronaut was chastised. He denied knowing the "meaning" of the flag. While the Confederate Battle Flag flew over many a battlefield during the South's fight for independence, modern-day liberals have designated the flag as a racist symbol. While the American flag flies just as prominently at KKK rallies and other white supremacist groups, only the Crimson Cross is selectively shown as the symbol for these radical groups.

The modern rise of the Crimson Cross has not been just at the International Space Station. That flag flew at Berlin when the wall came down and in Afghanistan as the Russians were driven out. It is an international symbol of opposition to oppression — something most Southerners should be very proud of. But in the globalist America Culture War where political correctness dominates the editors' pens and censorship, the Southern symbol is reviled.

Yet, every once in a while, in places you would not expect, there it is, snapping in the breeze.

And in an America, moving ever further from its origins, from the words and spirit of the Declaration of Independence and the original federalism, which recognized the states as the creator of the Union, the Confederate Battle Flag is like the roach the P.C. can't kill. It just keeps waving all across the South, and in many places outside of Dixie … even at the International Space Station! Look up at night, maybe you will see it.

Would not surprise me at all to see it in New Hampshire, though that won't be reported. How embarrassing — a symbol of liberty flying in such a place.

Why is there so much hatred towards the Confederate Battle Flag?

Why do so many of the ruling elite despise the Confederate Battle Flag?

One of these days you may be driving along an interstate highway and be surprised to see a huge garrison-sized Confederate Battle Flag flying proudly. These flags are part of the Sons of Confederate Veterans "Flags Across the South" program.

The crimson battle flag with a blue cross and thirteen white stars is the most recognized symbol of the South, the Civil War in America, and across the globe. In fact, if you think for a moment, does any other region in the United States have a symbol? Does the powerful Northeast? Does the West Coast? How about the Heartland? The answer is no.

Only the South has a regional symbol, and even a quasi-national anthem, *Dixie*.

Three decades ago these symbols flew at NASCAR race tracks, at many college and high school football games, and *Dixie* was played as a fight song for many schools.

But somewhere in the '80s the ruling elite decided these symbols of Southern regionalism and pride had to be erased. The excuse was they offended black Americans. They made every effort to associate the Confederate Battle Flag with raciest organizations. Slavery was embraced as the sole PC subject connected with the American Civil War.

Why?

Any real historian will tell you the only American slave ships which brought slaves to America flew the United States flag! The slave trade was condemned as illegal in the Confederate Constitution.

And once the US was created as a nation, the US flag flew over the harbors, North and

South, where slaves were brought to the United States. There was no Confederacy in those days, and there was no crimson battle flag.

So why is there so much hatred spewed against the battle flag of the Confederate Armed Forces? Why is the most recognized symbol of the South so viciously condemned?

Before I answer, let me ask another question. Do you know what the Stars and Bars looks like? No, not the crimson battle flag, the Stars and Bars. This was the first national flag of the Confederate States of America. The Stars and Bars kind of looks like the US flag. It has a red, white and red bar, with a blue field in the upper corner. Usually, it is seen with seven stars in a circle. Yep, that's the Stars and Bars. The Confederacy had two other national flags, one was a white sheet with a crimson battle flag in one corner, the third was a white sheet with a crimson battle flag in the corner, and red bar running from top to bottom on the other end.

OK, so let's talk about why the Confederate Flag is so hated?

The Confederate Battle Flag is a very attractive, recognizable flag. It is the most recognized symbol of the South. Across the globe, many oppressed people fly this flag as a symbol of resistance. It flew in Berlin when the Wall fell. It flew in Afghanistan when the Afghanis drove out the Soviets.

The Confederate Battle Flag makes Americans think about secession. It leads to discussions and questions about the principle of the "consent of the governed," and how that principle was completely ignored when Lincoln invaded the South. Before 1861 the legitimacy of the United States government rested on the sovereignty of the people and the fact that the states, as the representatives or agents of the people, joined the Union voluntarily. But that ended with secession. For whatever reason, thirteen Southern states chose to leave the Union. They left through democratic process and systems. The people of the state, either through referendum or through election of delegates to secession conventions, chose to leave the Union.

And when seven of those states joined together, they held a constitutional convention in Montgomery, Alabama, and drafted a new constitution with many important changes. In effect, the South created a new system for American governance.

The ultimate right of the people was asserted. The people of a state, if they did not wish to remain in the Union, could leave. If they did not want Obama Care, they could leave. If they did not support a war, they could leave. If they opposed Roe vs. Wade, or gay marriage, they could leave the Union.

It was this ability to secede peacefully, which acted as the single most effective restraint to the federal government overreaching itself.

The ruling elite despise the Confederate Battle Flag because of what it truly stands for — the original intent of the founding fathers in Philadelphia.

Take an opportunity during the Sesquicentennial to learn about America. Visit a local Sons of Confederate Veterans camp and learn about American history. We encourage people to read primary sources concerning the creation of the US Constitution and the actual events of secession in each of the Southern states. If you are armed with the facts of what really occurred, you might finally understand why there is such hatred towards the crimson battle flag.

Never more relevant; never more important!

The most well-known symbol of the South in the world, the Confederate Naval Ensign

---

At the First Battle of Manassas it became evident the resemblance of the First National Flag of the Confederacy and the Stars and Stripes confused an already chaotic battlefield environment. The similarity of the colors, combined with the real probability that regiments within the Confederate Army could be in blue or dark uniforms, required an immediate solution to a command and control problem on the modern battlefield. Something must be done. Too much was at stake to dawdle with committees, debates, long consideration.

The result was the creation of a battle flag, which would become globally renown as the symbol of a defiant Southern nation. The colors would span the globe as Captain Semmes and the CSS *Alabama* and twenty-seven other Confederate ocean-going raiders, along with blockade runners and merchantmen, travelled the high seas. The colors flew on the Pacific waters off the Asian mainland, in the Bering Sea, in the Indian Ocean, all over the Atlantic and in the Gulf of Mexico.

Here in America, the scarlet battle flag would embrace one design but many, many shades of red and pink, and even blue. The materials available across the South for the making of the flag were uncertain, the exact inks and dyes not always available. And the parochial individualism of commanders, states or regions within the South, would have an altering effect on the final product; so the color schemes could differ substantially. Pink battle flags were not uncommon. In the Trans-Mississippi theater, the battle flag would begin with a blue field. But the standard, the one the South grew to know and love, was the red field with a blue cross and white stars.

The purpose for the colors was always the same. The battle flag's design helped create an unmistakable, fear-creating presence on the battlefield. Combined with the rebel yell and the accuracy and unrelenting shock of Confederate infantry fire, a new Southern military identity on the battlefield was created. For commanders, it eased problems of command and control and reduced the number of friendly fire incidents. For the men in the *Gray Line*, it became their rallying point. The colors grew to become an emotional symbol which literally thousands of the most courageous and more noble within a unit would carry into fire. When mortally wounded, these Confederate heroes would, in their last breathe and effort, pass the colors on to a brother.

The Crimson Cross earned its place in the military history of the world and in American history. Riddled by ball and shot, drenched in the blood of their men, the colors of the South were born in the horror and glory of a war for Southern independence. More importantly, these colors participated in a desperate fight to preserve the Declaration of Independence and the original Constitution.

As a Southern soul born in a foreign land, New York, the colors were one of the very first things Southern I ever knew. I met them at a youthful age at the same time I met Marse Robert and Stonewall and became aware of Fort Sumter and states' rights. My Nana, raised by a one-legged veteran of Thomas Jackson's Corps, would tell of the heroic feats of men from Mecklenburg County, North Carolina. Similar stories were told to countless boys about their own heroes.

In my youth, the colors were everywhere, at NASCAR races, football games, parades and always at battlefields or on the covers of books. They hung on walls over the mantle in homes. No matter whether the author was of Southern persuasion or revisionist in his history or Yankee in his originality, the battle flag became a marketing symbol unparalleled when telling the story of the Southern struggle.

Across the planet the crimson cross would come to be known as the highly respected flag of the American Southland. And more, the flag would become a global rallying point for diverse peoples of many cultures who were engaged in fighting oppression, tyranny and occupation. Whether in Berlin when the Wall finally came down as the result of the quake of President Ronald Reagan or in Afghanistan when a defeated Soviet military Goliath withdrew behind its borders, the Confederate Battle Flag flew!

Over the past one-hundred-and-fifty years, the Confederate Flag has gained a global presence equal to symbols like the Christian cross. Possibly a handful of symbols are so recognized across the entire world. Companies like Coca Cola, McDonald's and Ford have literally spent billions of dollars to create a public presence equal to that of the Confederate Battle Flag.

And yet, some within the South, even within the Southern movement and the Sons of Confederate Veterans, want to distance themselves from this revered symbol of courage and liberty.

One must ask why?

I won't bother with the answers: they are the same as the ones you would hear on the battlefield at the first crack of a musket, when some would have to fill their canteen, or tie their shoe, or seize up.

Have the Confederate colors been misused, stolen by racist groups? Absolutely. Have our enemies and opponents taken advantage of the misuse of our colors to paint us, the South, with a racist brush? Most definitely! Should we seize the colors back, defend them as ours alone? Without question. These colors are the most recognized symbol of the South and resistance to oppression.

There is a real monetary value to the Confederate Flag in today's world. The initial investment in the creation of this symbol was the courage, blood sacrifice and defeat of our ancestors. But more has been invested. All the monuments constructed across the South with monies raised by the United Daughters of the Confederacy. All of the different ceremonies attended by tens of millions, if not hundreds of millions, over a span of one-hundred-and-fifty years to honor the *Cause* and those who perished for it.

The Confederate Flag has an immeasurable monetary value. It is world known and not likely to be forgotten in our lifetime or the foreseeable future. It has grown to become the symbol of the whole South, not just the soldiers who wore gray. If you are Southern, whether liberal or conservative, black or white, this flag is yours. It is how you are initially recognized around the world. Doesn't matter how much you protest it, doesn't matter what you think of it, a world of six billion people recognizes the colors as Dixie and the values of Dixie.

Our efforts should be towards defining the values the colors represent. We should condemn not only racism, but slavery as evil and a sin. If we argue today that only five percent of Southerners owned slaves, and that the South was attempting to end it on its own, and it would have ended without a war, then let's just take the next step and condemn it as you would condemn 50 million American abortions since Roe vs. Wade, or the tens of millions of Americans who use illegal drugs!

The Confederate States of America offered a different path for America. It offered a nation where God Himself was invited in the preamble of the CSA Constitution to provide His wisdom and protection to our nation. It offered an American nation, which could not be 17 trillion in debt because the governing mechanisms were there to prohibit a lunacy like that. The Confederate States of America offered an alternative America where each state molded and shaped itself independent of the others. South Carolinians knew this in 1860, and know it today.

The Confederate Battle Flag is not a relic to be placed in a museum behind glass. It is a living breathing symbol of individualism, Christianity, defiance of central authority, and a regional pride in a land called Dixie. It's known across the world, and running from it will not change that.

The defense of the battle flag may be the ultimate and initial step to fulfill the *Charge* we state at every meeting. And for me, the *Charge* is second only to my profession of faith said each Sunday at church. Just as I would always embrace my cross, so I would always drape myself in the colors.

Lastly, the flag is a rallying point, a safe place for all men of the South. It is a place of shade and respite. It is a place of history, but also a place where the future can be made. The colors tie together generations of family. From George Washington and Thomas Jefferson to today, the colors are the symbol of one people within the nation which flies the Stars and Stripes.

Section III

The Southern Movement Today

50 to 80 million Americans are descendants of a Confederate soldier!

What is the South in today's time and place?

Is there a Southern movement? Part I

Is there a Southern movement? Part II

50 to 80 million Americans are descendants of a Confederate soldier!

150 years after the War for Southern Secession, a conservative estimate would say one in six Americans are Southern by blood!

The numbers are stunning, but the formula to get them is pretty conservative.

First of all the estimate assumes 500,000 as the number of Confederate veterans who had children. This reflects half of the actual number of Southerners who served, close to one million. And though 300,000 died during the war, many could have had sizable families before the shots were fired at Ft. Sumter. Then one must estimate the number of children each veteran had. This estimate is six in the first post-veteran generation; from here to the next generation, and so on. We are presently in the sixth generation after the war. But if you only use five generations and the numbers of children per generation are as follows, six x five x four x four you come up with eighty million! Again, these numbers are based on half the number of men who fought for the South and one generation shy of what is living. So the estimate is fairly conservative.

Eighty million Americans could be descendants of Confederate soldiers who fought for the South in the Great War. If just one of your grandparents was born in the South, the odds are in your favor you are kin to a Confederate soldier!

Because of historical revisionism, the great tragedy of slavery and the mobility of the American public, interest in ancestry back to the time of the American war has faded somewhat. The Sons of Confederate Veterans, a heritage organization composed of lineal and collateral descendants of Confederate Veterans, is the largest Southern heritage organization with about thirty thousand members. The comparable Union organization is only about one fifth the size!

But with the Sesquicentennial Anniversary, interest is rising. And as more people begin to study why the nation divided, they may be stunned by the Southern accuracy in predicting the problems of America today. A study of the Confederate Constitution is worth the time because it is substantially different from the US Constitution in many ways. For example, in the Preamble, the Southern nation called for the protection and guidance of Almighty God. Thus the Confederates included God at the table of governance. This combined with a much less powerful central government all but eliminates the chance of a Roe vs. Wade decision in the South, and thus abortion would be illegal in the Southern nation. But other parts of the Southern Constitution prohibit bailouts for industry and earmarks for Congressmen. And lastly and most importantly, the Confederacy was caused by the third series of secession between the sovereign states and a higher government. The first secession came when the colonies left the British Empire. The second secession came when the original thirteen states individually withdrew from the Articles of Confederation to form the United States under the Constitution. And the third secession occurred when Southern states and territories formed the Confederacy. Secession would have been a recognized political act in a Southern nation, and thus would have placed a great restraint on overreach by the central government.

The issue of slavery has been an intellectual black hole in American schools when discussing the causes of secession. A study of early American politics and political theory and the events which led to secession, combined with the Confederate Constitution, point to many reasons for secession, not the least of which was a commitment to the original compact known as the Constitution. Limited government, the sovereignty of the states, and individual liberty were all fundamental to the Southern view of the Constitution. This constitution articulated an original view of the government:

Where government did not control and redistribute wealth, but rather sat as a neutral arbiter, concerned with fairness and providing opportunity to anyone willing to take it.

And a government where God was not only recognized but included in the process of the decision makers. Known as the Bible Belt, the South is still committed to the Christian God.

The Sesquicentennial Anniversary of the War for Southern Independence provides an opportunity to look at an alternative form of American democracy, one where the states retained the power position, the central government formed for defense and interstate commerce purposes only. And since so many of the American population today are related to the men who served the South under arms, it might be time to take a look at what they were fighting for, and not be blinded by the one issue, which certainly was a black mark for all involved — the Europeans and Northerners who brought the slaves to America and sold them to the South, and then purchased the products produced on Southern plantations. There is enough fault for all when discussing slavery, but there are other issues which could help us find our way to the future.

What is the South in today's time and place?

Many Southern spokesmen talk of a different path, but what is it?

Southern heritage — what is it in today's world?

There are a number of Southern patriots, like the Kennedy brothers, Tim Manning, the men who attend the Southern National Congress, and some members of the Sons of Confederate Veterans and ladies of the United Daughters of the Confederacy and others who profess that there is a "Southern nation" or point of view even to this day. And while I wish it were so, I find little real evidence of an alternate American view peculiar to the South. There is no doubt there are two different views within the US and it is divided. But these two different views are national in nature and not regional.

The South of 1861 was very different from the rest of the Union. Slavery was the single most obvious difference prior to secession. But that difference was like the tip of an iceberg, it was the visible part of a vast societal difference. The differences between the Union and the South were articulated in the Confederate Constitution. These differences, when combined, offered an alternative trail for American democracy and Americana. But alas, the war of conquest and victory ended that brief sojourn down a different path.

Still the South retained its identity for about a century after Appomattox. The South remained a primarily rural and agricultural society. The South's culture blossomed as the only means of regional expression. Music, food, religion and conservative politics were as different from the other parts of the nation as its dialects. And of course, the history of the war and its remembrance of the men who led and fought the war, epitomized what a Southerner was. Military colleges like The Citadel and Virginia Military Institute dotted the South and preserved the Southern martial tradition. And the unique aspects of its separate states continued to develop. No one could confuse the people of Cajun country of Louisiana for those of the Shenandoah Valley or Austin for Charleston.

Politically, the South was the geographic core of the Democratic Party for a long time after the war, but eventually the entire region shifted to the Republican Party when the Democrats embraced secularism and socialism. Even as late as the turn of the 21st century, the South still united in presidential contests and elected some of the nation's most conservative senators and congressmen.

The Bible Belt, though depleted some by the invasion of foreigners, still includes a Christian God in daily life and the church is still a major center of social life in many places in Dixie. But with the Civil Rights movement, and more importantly, the widespread use of air conditioning (which allowed the descendants of Yankee conquerors to settle and stay in the South), and the development, nationalization and globalization of electronic communications equipment (the television, radio and personal computer), the South was finally overwhelmed and is being assimilated into a centralized milquetoast America.

And still I must ask, what is Southern today? I look for it. Like an old man going through a dimly lit attic, I pick up old dusty artifacts of my life and look under them for the South. I walk the town square looking for evidence of a Southern economy or aspects of Southern capitalism and don't seem to find them. Occasionally, I will find handmade goods or jams and fruits canned at home. But there are no Southern products which reflect a Southern pride and self-sufficiency.

Are Southerners more dedicated to God? Possibly, but would a modern Southern nation invite God to the governing table as the Confederacy did in its Preamble to the Constitution? Would our Christianity govern our air waves, removing the foul language we hear every day on the radio, and the soft porn we see on our televisions? Would the South ban abortion and protect traditional marriage? Are we more honorable men?

Do we turn away government subsidies and benefits? Do we practice Christian charity in business? Do we see land, agriculture and natural resource development as our *national* means of making of living?

Do we believe in Virginian George Washington's warnings of avoiding international treaties and alliances? Or is the Southern commitment to Israel too great and thus we would be as engaged in international affairs as America today? Would our Southern nation be a member of the United Nations?

Do Southerners still see individual liberty as the most important political priority? And do we see a centralized government as the most dangerous threat to that individual liberty? Would a Southern nation have Social Security and an Environmental Protection Agency? Do we still see the state as the sovereign founder of a confederated central government, and if yes, how would that manifest itself in a world that seems to be consolidated and centralizing?

As a child, when I studied the South, I could see clear differences between the South and the rest of the nation. I could see a land, a people unto itself. I could see smallness as a good thing. I could see the aristocracy, which ran the South though I did not like that part of the South. I could see the belief in the ownership of land as the ultimate source of wealth. I could see a people who let time and progress pass in order to live a life focused on God, family, nature and culture. I could see a proud unity across the South, which is not there today. Differences over the Confederate Battle Flag and the retreat from *Dixie* are only symptoms of a broader rejection of regional identity and independence.

I don't write this to demean the South or its present-day patriots. I write it simply to ask the question: What is the South today and is it really different from the failing United States? Secession may be the eventual political outcome of a federal government drunk with the national credit card and an inability to say no. But that secession is not one based in a regional difference, but in an economic reality that the golden goose is barren of any future fruit.

I wish there were a South — a South where men and women had clearly different roles and those roles were based on the design of God. I wish there were a South where honor, real honor had meaning. I wish there was a united South of black and white, where our mutual history, respect for each other and common needs made us one Southern people. So minds of the South, if there is a unique South in this day and time, write about it, define it! Southern writers and thinkers, make us aware of today's regionalism. Don't look too far back to find that definition. Either it is here and now or it is not.

And if there is not a here and now South, then let us consider creating a better people first and nation second. Clearly the evils, which are destroying the nation known as the United States, were predicted by the founding fathers. The US is collapsing because of its people. While they may blame their politicians, they blame them because they actually desire magicians in Congress. America's people want elected officials who can fund their parochial causes without raising taxes or running up deficits.

The politicians have used this greed at the grassroots level to erode the Constitution. Clearly the court has reversed the meaning of words. The history of the United States proves how fragile the visions and words of one generation are. Time is like a great eroding chemical which removes the shine of the brilliance of the past. It is time for a new generation, one looking for a Christian nation where right and wrong are defined in the Bible, and where the tax collector of today is as unwelcome as the tax collector of biblical times.

Can the South regain its place in time? Can we develop our regional identify before the national crisis which destroys the US occurs so that when it happens we know who we are and what we want?

Battle rages in central Virginia, echoes of the Civil War

An important part of the Culture War has erupted in Richmond and Appomattox, Virginia. And it may be awakening a Southern titan … maybe not.

Richmond and Appomattox, Virginia, are presently sites for one heck of a battle between Southerners over the flying of Confederate colors.

Taking their cue from ABC News and other *objective* mainstream news organizations which believe they should not wear the United States flag on their lapels when they report the news, some Southerners in positions of authority are refusing to fly Confederate colors at historic places like the Museum of the Confederacy and a chapel once used by Confederate Veterans housed in an old soldiers' home.

Richmond, Virginia, is also the site of a battle between the Department of Veterans of Affairs and the Sons of Confederate Veterans concerning the proper honors for between twelve and fourteen thousand Confederate veterans who are entitled to headstones to be provided by the Veterans Administration. And in the Shenandoah Valley, the city of Lexington, home of the remains of both Stonewall Jackson and Robert E. Lee, has changed its policies concerning the flying of the various Confederate Flags on city property. Lexington is the home of Washington-Lee University and Virginia Military Institute. It is one of the most hallowed sites in the entire South.

These culture war battles are a continuation of previous actions in Georgia, South Carolina and Texas, which began in the late eighties, early nineteen nineties to marginalize the Southern presence. Times have changed since the 100th Anniversary of the American Civil War when the nation, under John F. Kennedy, took great pains to honor the South. Not this time.

This time the Sesquicentennial Anniversary (150th) has been turned into a nationwide opportunity to shame the South, dishonor those who served the South and sweep as much American history as possible under the rug.

The national leadership of the United Daughters of the Confederacy appears to be complicit in the ongoing actions to hide the Confederate colors in Richmond. And Waite Rawls, a graduate of Virginia Military Institute, member of the Sons of Confederate Veterans and director of the Museum of the Confederacy, has been the spokesperson for the museum explaining the reasons for not flying the Confederate Flag at Appomattox. Pointing to reunification as the result of Appomattox, Rawls has said it would not be appropriate to fly the colors there.

However, the national leadership of the Sons of Confederate Veterans has finally been awakened to the ongoing struggles. The national board of directors of the Sons of Confederate Veterans recently passed a resolution calling on its membership to boycott the grand opening of a new annex of the Museum of the Confederacy at Appomattox, while simultaneously calling on the museum to fly one Confederate Flag at the new site.

And in a letter to the 30,000 members of the Sons of Confederate Veterans, Michael Givens has begun the process to rally his forces for an extended fight. But Givens knows the membership of the SCV has proven to be an unreliable political force. Last summer when Givens called on the various state organizations of the SCV to act in support of Virginia concerning the headstones at Oakwood Cemetery, the reaction was not all it could have been.

A few hardcore leaders in Texas attempted to organize a mail campaign to federal elected officials to make them aware of the VA's failure to meet the law passed in Congress. Texas had the potential to generate 10,000 letters from its members. But another group of leaders within the Texas SCV (known as grannies) blocked that mail offensive and only a pitiful 400 letters were sent from Texas. Texas had been in the national news concerning vanity license plates, but the Texas SCV folded its colors when Governor Perry dismissed their application.

So this new effort by the Sons of Confederate Veterans under Michael Givens will be a real test of the membership. Will the membership rally across the South to support the *Cause* or will they follow the lead of the Texas grannies and let political correctness rule the day?

Givens is organizing things using the most modern communication technologies. He is a proven leader and communicator and will be breaking new ground in coordinating efforts across Dixie. If Givens can rally a large segment of the 30,000 members there may be a new voice in the Culture War in America.

Interestingly, the catalyst for all this activity is disaffected local members of the United Daughters of the Confederacy and Sons of Confederate Veterans who were tired of inaction by the large heritage organizations. Susan Hathaway has risen to an important leadership role in this ongoing heritage battle. But she insists there are many involved and she is only one of many who want to see appropriate honors to the ancestors who sacrificed all for home and hearth.

For more information about the modern Southern movement, visit the Confederate War College and read "Is there a Southern Movement in America?"

Is there a Southern movement? Part I

2012 is one heck of a year, no doubt a crossroads year! So is the South preparing to bolt?

Is there a Southern movement within the complex diverse cultural quilt that is America as we head towards November of 2012? Is there any reason to think the South is what it was, a region of its own values and political, social and economic interests?

I define the Southern movement as people who see present-day values in:

Both the original Constitution, as written by the Founders, and in the actions of the people of the South to try to maintain the original political structure of their nation and a desire to bring those elements into today's political discourse;

Loyalty to the South, second only to a Christian God;

The concept of republic and the legal, accepted right of secession.

To be a movement, it must be concerned with today, with the challenges of today, with the politics of today, with the future. This is an essential part of the question and is the standard by which we will measure whether there is a present-day movement.

The movement may be enhanced and, to some extent, evidenced through culture and music. The Southern tradition is about a love of the land, and the place of Christ in daily living. Any Southern movement would not be about the dust of history, but about the needs of today and the application of the principles, values and character of the men who were the South of 1860.

This article is intended to explore the size and condition of the Southern Movement, if there is one. Is it coordinated or operating along separate and uncooperative avenues? Is the Southern movement engaged in the Culture War? If so, how? Is the South ashamed of its history? Has the most recent invasion of Yankees to the South, in the post-air conditioning era, overwhelmed Southern identity? Or is the South resisting the homogenization of regions within the United States into a sort of a milquetoast Americanism?

Is it coincidence, or part of a divine plan that the United States of America is experiencing the Sesquicentennial (150th) remembrance of its Civil War at the same time the nation is at a crossroads as big as the one at Fort Sumter?

It's important to note here that Southern symbols, icons and culture were still alive and well as late as the 1970s. Confederate naval ensigns would fly at high school and college football games and decorate cars burning gas on the various NASCAR tracks throughout the South. Rebels was a common mascot name for high school or college sports teams. *Dixie* would play as often as the national anthem. And Southern icons like Lee and Jackson were still hung in portraits over the bed of a family's son(s).

Southern bands like Alabama continued into the late twentieth century. Groups like Shenandoah offered hope that Southern music would survive. But modern country just isn't what it was. Southern rock and roll doesn't dominate the radio stations of Dixie any more.

Somewhere and somehow, these regional trademarks were erased or marginalized. The culture war of the sixties continues to this day. Inclusion of some has meant exclusion of others. This has not been about making room at the table for more, but about pushing some out of their seats, so that others could occupy them.

As I researched this article, I tried to look at the widest possible view of what could be considered a part of the Southern movement. One commercial business seemed a real possibility as a participant in the movement. This business uses the Confederate naval ensign and the words Dixie and Southern in its name. Yet, when I contacted them for an interview, the reply was startling. They did not want to be interviewed or mentioned in this article! They did not want to offend anyone's feelings. I found it confusing they would so blatantly use Southern symbols to adorn their business, yet refuse an interview for this article.

Let me close the introduction by saying that just because a group or person is mentioned in this article does not indicate they are a part of a Southern movement, but rather through my experience and knowledge I felt addressing them in this paper was important. And there may be groups dedicated to modern application of Southern values which are not mentioned because of my limited knowledge. Should those groups see this article and wish to be included in any further work in this area, I hope you will contact me.

Jed Marum

Let's begin this article with a little known, but very talented musician and song writer whose upbringing was in Boston, Massachusetts. Jed Marum moved to Texas for employment reasons. But as things turned out, he has gone farther and farther down the road of songwriter and entertainer. His music is Celtic and also Southern. Yes, that's what I said, Southern.

One of Jed's best songs is titled *I Didn't Know I was a Yankee, 'til I Moved to Texas!* Jed is fascinated by the South, its story, and the tragedy it has endured as a result of Yankee invasion and occupation. Jed's music tells the story of the South from the Southern view. He is operating in the underground which is the Southern movement. He performs for living history and reenactment events and at meetings of heritage organizations. He has written songs and music for movies about the Civil War.

Jed is unique, both in his talent and in his vantage point. Because he is not Southern, Jed appreciates the South as only a foreigner can.

The Heart of the Movement

The very heart of what is the movement, if there is a movement, is an ill-defined but beautiful concept known as *the South*. This concept, to my knowledge, has never been succinctly described. But attempts have been made.

One attempt dealt solely with the contest in Virginia and two of the South's icons, Robert E. Lee and Thomas Jonathan Jackson. This effort was a video program produced by New Liberty Videos www.newlibertyvideo.com of Missouri titled *Warriors of Honor*. This story paints a picture of the martial South, which wraps together a deep and shared Christian faith which pervaded the leadership of the Army of Northern Virginia with a devotion to duty, a conduct of honor, and brilliance on the field unparalleled in American history.

The South is more than the Army of Northern Virginia. The South's ideals and essence were described through the creation of the Confederate Constitution and the great courage and sacrifice made by so many. Alas, there were lesser beings in the South white population, and these men's blood flows today, just as that of the nobler men. The great individualism, which is a Southern trait, also created fissures and fractures which divided the South through crisis, as it does today.

Still, there was a higher South — a land before heaven on earth. The Confederate naval ensign is a symbol of this South. It is a rally point for Southern pride, for Southern nationalism, and a reminder of the Constitution of Madison's hand and Jefferson's Declaration. The Confederate naval ensign is an internationally known symbol of the South. With respect to its value as a regional trademark, it would be impossible to estimate in terms of dollars. This flag represents the defiance of the South as it left the Union, and could be the symbol of a modern Southern movement.

Heritage Organizations

Any exploration of a Southern movement would be incomplete without consideration of the various heritage organizations which trace themselves back to the Confederacy. These are the largest identifiable groups connected to the South. The largest of these organizations, the Sons of Confederate Veterans (SCV), is somewhere between 25,000 and 28,000 members. Headquartered in Columbia, Tennessee, its membership extends overseas to Brazil (where a Confederate colony was established after the war) and in Europe. Though their *Charge* (purpose) is to vindicate the *Cause*, they are not organized, nor do they conduct activities which would do so. They have no political arm and their fund-raising efforts are anemic. Their sole strength is at the local level in towns and hamlets across the South.

As a member of the Sons of Confederate Veterans since 1994, I first became aware of the different heritage organizations of the South. Foremost among these is the United Daughters of the Confederacy (UDC). It is not difficult to say that this group, more than any other, is responsible for most of the monuments and preservation of many of the battle colors and documents of the Confederate South. However, in recent times, the UDC has established a series of hurdles to membership which would fatigue most marathon runners. Similar to the SCV, a genealogical connection from a Confederate veteran to a potential member is required. But proof of that reality is in some sense beyond normal standards, and other personal information requested could cause potential members to hesitate in their application.

Another organization, much smaller and of dubious commitment to the Southern Cause, is the Military Order of the Stars and Bars. The MOS&B is not large and seems to have a belief in the genetic properties of leadership, whereby the descendants of the great Southern leaders of one-hundred-and-fifty years ago have somehow secured the leadership traits of the South's most renowned heroes and will exercise them to control today's lesser beings.

Other auxiliary groups like the Descendants of Confederate Veterans and the Order of the Confederate Rose are more evidence of fissures and fractures within established heritage organizations than a rush by the general public to join the Southern movement. Recruiting efforts by these organizations have targeted existing heritage organization memberships rather than break ground into new, untilled areas for membership.

Of course, the Sons of Confederate Veterans is the premier Southern heritage organization with membership just under thirty thousand. (It is not growing despite the Sesquicentennial Anniversary.) Disappointing, given that a genealogical formulae developed by Dr. Ray James of Texas A & M and some of his colleagues, indicates there may be as many as 80 million living American descendants of the Confederacy.

Across the South, the Sons of Confederate Veterans is probably the most active group concerning Southern heritage. While they do not participate in influencing government policy, they are very active at the camp (local) level in parades, classrooms and conducting ceremonies honoring their Confederate ancestry. They do maintain a presence, a Southern presence in thousands of cities and villages across the South. Many of their members and some of their leadership are devoted to the *Charge* and the *Cause*. So the verdict is still out. They do much, but with the right leadership, a change in attitude of a segment of this organization and a modernizing of their Constitutions, they could become a real force in the movement.

The Internet's Role in the Southern movement

The Internet plays a big role in the modern 21st century Southern movement. It provides a whole new, international means to link people of a Southern attitude. Interestingly, if you were to use Google to search the internet for the word "Dixie," you would find 103,000,000 hits. If you search for the term "Yankee," you find 23,000,000 hits! A startling discovery.

The most common use of the Internet in the Southern movement is for websites. These sites normally act as advertisements for the local organizations, camps of the Sons of Confederate Veterans. There are also sites for museums, battlefields, reenactor units, etc.

Other communication devices used on the Internet are e-mail lists. Individuals or groups become news gatherers for events and issues occurring in the South. Some of these lists can have thousands of members and are a means for quickly distributing information across the South. The Sons of Confederate Veterans Telegraph is an e-mail list run from their national headquarters in Columbia, Tennessee. In addition, a blog is also operated by the SCV.

The Southern Heritage News and Views is both a website and a news distribution point with more than 3,500 subscribers. Charles Demastus, the owner, has been operating this outlet for fourteen years and reports subscribers from all over the world. Mr. Demastus reports the subscriber list for Southern Heritage News and Views has leveled out over the past couple of years. Given we are in the second year of the Sesquicentennial, one has to ask if the poor economy has cooled enthusiasm? Or does the leveling off reflect reaching the ceiling of people interested in Southern or Civil War history?

One of the venues featuring Southern culture on the internet is a new brand of radio. This radio operates strictly off the Internet.

One of those radio stations is Dixie Radio, www.dixieradio.net owned and operated by Winston Boulware of Millbrook, Alabama. Winston says: "I do it for the fun of it."

Social media like Facebook have created a national network for people who enjoy Southern culture and/or participate in Civil War reenactments, cotillions, balls and living histories. There are a number of Southern Facebook pages set up, each with hundreds or thousands of members.

It is a theory of mine that the personal computer has done a lot to create a whole new wave of authors of varying talents, intellectual skills and academic training. You need only attend SCV reunions each year to see new authors with new stories and theories. While much of this is probably not central to the development of a Southern movement, some seed may sprout from this wild garden which could ignite increased interest.

African-American Confederates

When asked about the diversity of the subscribers connected to Southern Heritage News and Views, Charles pointed to H.K. Edgerton, Al McCray and Bob Harrison as long-time subscribers of African-American descent.

Mr. Edgerton is especially well known as a spokesman for his pro-Confederate views. Recently his brother, Lee, sent out an e-mail announcement about a book he had just completed concerning H.K.'s famous walk. "On October 14, 2002, H.K. and I set off to bring attention to the wrongful removal of the Confederate plaques from the G.S.A. Building in Austin, Texas. This endeavor is now known as The March Across Dixie. We covered seven states and dozens of cities in this endeavor."

Lee Edgerton refers to a despicable act by then Governor George Bush in ordering the removal of plaques acknowledging the financial contributions of the United Daughters of the Confederacy to build a state building. Bush's orders were executed in the dark of night to prevent public notice or action. As is the SCV *modus operandi*, they took the state to court, but failed to get the plaques restored to their original location. However Mr. Edgerton's heroic efforts made him a hero within the Southern movement. For more information about the book, *The Historical March Across Dixie, 2002-2003* (Copywriter 2011), call 828-505-1385. This coffee table book is filled with colorful photos of the march.

In a telephone interview with H.K., I found him impassioned, highly educated, articulate, experienced in celebrating Southern culture and history, and committed to his purpose. H.K. said the enemies of the South "divided the South white and black. The whites who owned my ancestors were not just called master, but family and friend."

H.K. said he had been invited by a Black and Latino student organization at Wright State University to speak to them. When asked what he was going to speak about, he said, "I am going to talk about the African-American contribution to the war effort as soldiers, teamsters, and operating the plantations and the rest of the home front while the whites were off to war."

He went on, "They are trying to erase the memory of what we did to help the South, and to take away our position of honor in the South." H.K. mentioned a black soldier who served with Confederate Cavalry leader Nathan Bedford Forrest.

Some within the Southern movement talk about secession and the creation of a new Southern nation. I asked H.K. how that fit into his work and thinking. "That is not part of my agenda," he said. "It's scary to think about that. But people are tired of the tyranny. The South is still under Reconstruction. Each time they attack the Confederate naval ensign, or like Governor Bush taking down the plaques, we see occupation." H.K. made a point to thank the League of the South for the many times they have helped him on projects.

H.K. was 55 years old when he did his march across the South. But that wasn't his last walk. H.K. mentioned leading a Martin Luther King Parade carrying the Confederate Flag and walking with the Sons of Confederate of Veterans in Cross City, Florida.

For more information on H.K. Edgerton go to www.southernheritage411.com H.K. calls himself a "seven-day-a-week Confederate!"

Another African-American very active in the Sons of Confederate Veterans is Nelson Wimbush who has attended many national reunions. I first met Nelson in 1996 in Richmond at the 100th Reunion of the SCV.

Race is not the issue reported in the mainstream media. The present modern-day Southern movement accepts the equality of civil rights. The League of the South, the most ardent of the groups within the Southern movement, states: "The LS disavows a spirit of malice and extends an offer of good will and cooperation to Southern blacks in areas where we can work together as Christians to make life better for all people in the South. We affirm that, while historically the interests of Southern blacks and whites have been in part antagonistic, true Constitutional government would provide protection to all law-abiding citizens …"

In fact, serious research and academic work focused on the contributions to the Southern war effort by African-Americans are sought after and highly prized. Whether it be on the battlefield, serving as soldiers or as combat support and combat service support troops constructing trench lines or driving the supply wagons operating with the armies, or at home, running the plantations, it is becoming more evident each year that the South's African-American population was essential to sustaining the war effort.

Abbeville Institute

Abbeville Institute http://abbevilleinstitute.org in South Carolina is certainly one of the intellectual centers of the Southern movement. The Institute holds annual conferences on various aspects of the politics of regional differences and events which led to secession. Every year a summer program for college and graduate students is conducted at the Institute. Members see their charge as that of illuminating vast areas of history that clearly indicate the vindictive and aggressive actions of the North against the South.

Dr. Don Livingston wrote me after a telephone interview to say: "The Institute was formed in 2003 by 12 academics at the University of Virginia concerned that the Southern tradition is no longer being taught in colleges and universities across the South except as fuel for political correctness. The task of the Institute is to critically explore what is true and valuable in the Southern tradition. To this end, it holds an annual week-long summer school for college and graduate students and an annual scholars conference for academics and other thoughtful people. To examine what is valuable in the Southern tradition is at the same time to present a critique of much of American modernity.

"The Institute, from its small beginning, now has more than 120 academics associated with its mission. These scholars, during the past decade, have produced more than 40 scholarly books on all aspects of the Southern tradition. The scholarship of the Institute is necessarily thought provoking. Readers are invited to rethink the nationalist and other paradigms that determine so much of American culture."

As an example, consider this from a recent conference on the topic of Northern dissent from Lincoln's war: "Nationalist historians for 150 years have protected Americans from confronting the stark immorality of prosecuting what French philosopher Bertrand de Jouvenel called, 'a war such as Europe had never yet seen' to force eleven States into a federation from which their people had voted to secede. Should eleven American States secede today and form a federation of their own, such a war would be judged criminal."

In a telephone interview, Dr. Donald Livingston described the Southerners of Sumter as "bearing witness to the Jeffersonian view of the Constitution. We see the Southern tradition as looking all the way back to the original Constitution. The South is older than the United States. It had an identity that was recognized before the Constitution was written."

The Institute's goals express an understanding of present bias and establish an over-the-horizon objective: "This condition in higher education is not going to change overnight. Those who created it are tenured and will dominate in higher education for at least a generation — and even longer since they are disposed to hire and tenure only their own. Even so, there are many scholars in America and abroad who take inspiration from the Southern tradition and many others who are open to what it has to teach. Students too are open. Many feel they are somehow encountering on campus a profound intellectual and spiritual disorder, but they do not know how to think about it."

The Abbeville Institute is on the cutting edge of bringing the Southern view up to today. Its most recent book is *Rethinking the American Union for the 21st Century*. (Pelican Publishing, 2012). It can't get more challenging and timely than that.

The Institute also conducts Jefferson Seminars, local gatherings to explore a topic guided by an Institute scholar. If you would like to fund one for your community, contact the Institute at contactus@abbevilleinstitute.org.

The Grady McWhiney Research Foundation
www.mcwhiney.org/mission.html

This not-for-profit foundation is focused on the study of the history of the mid-19th century United States, Civil War, American military affairs and Texas history. Dr. Grady Mc-

Whiney, the founder of this foundation, had a very pro-Southern reputation.

A well-known and respected scholar, McWhiney served as head of the Southern History Institute at the University of Alabama for many years. His published work, in the form of several books and numerous articles, has been both ground-breaking and provocative. In the course of his nearly forty years as a professional historian, McWhiney earned a reputation for impeccable scholarship which often led to unconventional insights into our nation's history." Dr. McWhiney earned his Ph.D at Columbia University in New York.

Dr. McWhiney did serious work in the study and consideration of General Braxton Bragg, CSA and also Southern history. "His most path-breaking and provocative work, *Cracker Culture: Celtic Ways in the Old South*," is directly taken from the website page describing Dr. McWhiney. So one would think the Foundation is deeply involved in the preservation of a positive Southern history.

Dr. Don Frazier, president and CEO of McWhiney, has been with the foundation for twenty years. He says the "foundation is open to more interpretation, advancing investigation and scholarship in Southern history," and went on to say they had published a lot of Civil War books over the years.

Dr. Frazier said that McWhiney's work in *Cracker Culture* focused on "the Celtic influence in the formation of the Southern culture." Frazier went on to say more work is needed to continue to develop that theme.

Dr. Frazier indicated the South had been a brake on evolving the Constitution away from a Republic towards centralization. He used the term "obstructionist" to describe how the Southern senators and congressmen had slowed the process until secession. Once their chairs were empty, Lincoln and the remaining Congress were able to begin the process, which has brought this nation to its present condition.

As a professor in the field for more than twenty years, Dr. Frazier believes the Southern movement may have "reached its crest and is now subsiding. Part of what they are arguing for has been co-opted by the Libertarian movement and other groups nationally. In many ways, what they had been saying were regional (Southern) concerns but now are becoming national concerns. There is a general uneasiness with what is occurring at the national level."

Lastly, Dr. Frazier said Southerners had made a huge tactical mistake by not condemning racism. Because they would not separate themselves from racism in the post-war years, their credibility on other issues, and the future of the American society was suspect.

The Stephen D. Lee Institute

The Stephen D. Lee Institute www.stephendleeinstitute.com is part of the educational arm of the Sons of Confederate Veterans. The purpose of the Institute is described on its website: "The Institute's goal is to organize accomplished and distinguished professional scholarship to inform our members and the general public of the Southern side of the war. To that end the Institute makes available recognized scholars to present such subjects as states' rights and the Constitutional aspects of the war; economic motives for invasion of the South; the dubious benevolence behind the slavery issue; Union Army war crimes and other unsavory aspects of the war against the South in 1861-1865; and other aspects of the true causes and nature of the war."

Brag Bowling, current chairman of the Stephen D. Lee Institute, said "We are trying to give a solid academic foundation to the cause of the Southern secession. A lot of people realize that the Stephen D. Lee Institute is becoming an educational force." Morris Dees of the Southern Poverty Law Center, an arch enemy of the South, called the S. D. Lee Institute the "Confederate think tank."

The Stephen D. Lee Institute convenes in locations around the South bringing academic expertise of great renown together to address questions important to the Constitutional crisis of 1859-1860. Many leaders within the SCV believe the past struggle has great relevance to what is occurring within the United States today. The next session of the Stephen D. Lee Institute will be conducted in Chattanooga, Tennessee, February 7-8, 2014.

The Kennedy Twins

Intellectual pursuits are not just the possession of institutes. Two of the most powerful intellects in the Southern movement are the Kennedy brothers, Donnie and Ron. Their book, *The South Was Right!*, has sold thousands of copies, and is must reading for many in the Southern movement. With this book, sold on the shelves of Barnes and Noble, the South crossed sabers with the politically correct version of history. And if the Kennedys' writings are electrifying, their ability to communicate from the *pulpit* is an even stronger weapon.

Donnie Kennedy said, "I wonder is there a Southern movement? But as compared to the past, there is so much more now … in a broad sense, there must be a Southern movement. The Abbeville Institute is an excellent example of the growth of it in my life time. It's hard to define, hard to prove it. The Southern movement is in the heart, but not in the Yellow Pages."

Donnie and Ron became Southern nationalists in the late sixties.. But today Donnie says that Facebook is filled with references to a Southern movement. "In the sixties we felt like we were by ourselves, but today we see a lot more evidence of people who feel as we do."

Don Kennedy sees the same trends as Dr. Frazier, but from a much more optimistic perspective. Kennedy believes because Southern views have become more popular at a national level, this should encourage local people in the South to coalesce around a Southern identity. "Now at last we are seen as the wave of the future. Everything that we have said as Southern nationalists is coming to fruition. We have allies now! We are celebrating!"

Ron and Don are looking for a *Ron Paul* for the Southern national movement. That was the whole reason for the Kennedy effort to get into the Republican primary movement four years earlier. "One day there will be a standard bearer for the South. Ron Paul is setting an example for the future. Just as the Libertarians have had to wait their turn; but it came, so will the turn of the South!"

Kennedy sees the Southern movement as the best answer for America when it collapses under the great financial strains being created by the socialists in Washington and at the state capitals. "We must have a plan, a vision of where to go when the United States collapses."

Many museums in the South have had to redefine themselves in order to qualify for money. In Columbus, Georgia, a museum dedicated to the Confederate Navy had to reorganize itself as the Civil War Naval Museum in order to qualify for federal monies. Jefferson Davis' prediction that the winners would write the history seems even truer today than it did in the years immediately following the war. Many Southern leaders wrote memoirs and histories. These writings could not be twisted by the victors. But they are less and less available.

Sea Raven Press

There are a number of publishers who seem to have a connection with the Southern movement. Pelican Publishing in New Orleans, Louisiana, may be the largest and most recognizable, but they are not the only ones. Eastern Digital Resources on the East Coast and Sea Raven Press in central Tennessee are two small publishers who seek out and publish less well-known writers.

Cassidy Ravensdale, is the president of Sea Raven Press, www.searavenpress.com. Ms. Ravensdale said they "believe that Sea Raven Press is the world's number one pro-South publisher." Lochlainn Seabrook is their primary author and has been writing for more than fifteen years, averaging about one book a year. He is presently working on a children's book. *A Rebel Born: A Defense of Nathan Bedford Forrest* was awarded the Jefferson Davis Historical Gold Medal by the United Daughters of the Confederacy.

When I asked Ms. Ravensdale if the term "Southern movement" meant anything to her, she immediately became animated in her voice. She responded, "Over the past 150 years there have been a lot of Northerners and misinformed Southerners who know little about Southern culture, the causes for secession and the war. Mr. Seabrook is a truth teller who wants to get the truth out through his writings." She went on to say that the Southern movement is about preserving the Southern culture in all its truth and beauty.

Sea Raven Press is associated with the League of the South, and Mr. Seabrook's work has been commended by Michael Givens, present commander of the Sons of Confederate Veterans.

Sea Raven Press is located in Middle Tennessee in Franklin. They sell their books through a wide variety of local vendors that include both gun shops and hairdressers, and through a variety of larger distributors and bookstore chains. When asked about the Southern movement in relations to book sales, Ms. Ravensdale said, "Our sales our doubling every six months!"

Mr. Seabrook also writes both country and blue grass music and is related to Elvis Presley and other country and bluegrass artists.

Reenactors

One very large group of men who could comprise sizeable elements within the Southern movement are reenactors. These men are mostly formed in small company-sized unit, and have invested money and time in developing themselves as reenactors. They practice the skills necessary to perform as period correct reenactors. Their kit, uniform, weapons, tentage and accessories can easily run more than a thousand dollars. Then there is the cost of travel to far-off places and possibly the expense of taking off work or at least using vacation days. Reenactments are not weather sensitive. Rain or cold, wind or extreme heat can be the environment one could be exposed to for days. So there is a level of commitment to being a reenactor.

For the larger battles, like Gettysburg, Shiloh and others, thousands of men will travel hundreds of miles. Some will bring horses and cannon. At Gettysburg, it is not unusual to have more than 10,000 reenactors, sometimes as many as 20,000, to refight the famous campaign.

However, the motives for reenacting are diverse and because there are literally hundreds, possibly thousands of Southern reenactor units, it would be impossible to say that even a good-sized segment of the men are members of the Southern movement.

A lot of the reenactors have an interest in history, and probably a majority do it because of brothers, friends, etc. who are involved, and they love the camaraderie. Les Pettigrew, captain of the 15th Texas: "Camaraderie is the glue that keeps it all together. Taking care of each other is a large part of the experience and does help to meld you into a cohesive unit." Les expects to put thirty rifles in the field at the 150th Anniversary of Shiloh.

"We sit around campfires at night and talk about the history of the war." In a way, a lot of reenactors do it for patriotism of the South. Do some have political preferences? All reenactors have their own opinion, but everybody is still for the Southland.

In response to a question about the Southern movement, Captain Pettigrew said; "Regarding the Southern movement, I think most Southern reenactors would like to see preservation of Southern values, but there are many ways to do that."

Museums, churches, odds and ends

Some not sensitive to the nuances of social intellectual fashion might think the many Civil War round tables which are scattered over the nation are an element within the Southern movement. But alas, they are not. While they do have Southerners as a portion of their membership, the round tables are more a market for college professors peddling their propaganda than they are an expression of Southern culture.

Modern American academic fashion has swung obscenely to the side of minorities, placing huge amounts of emphasis on the abstracts of history, rather than focusing on its main elements. Diversity has shattered reality as kids learn more about the eccentricities of a time than they do about the major philosophical and political developments of an era. This is most evident in Civil War museums where more and more space is being occupied by the sideshows of the era. Titanic figures like Jefferson Davis, Robert E. Lee, Thomas Jackson and so many others are pushed aside to make room for the stories of slaves, women, or other novelties of the era. And while the story of slavery is an essential part of the era and of the story, the story is broader than the fashion of today. For example, there were 3.5 million slaves in a South where the population was around nine million. Had the African-American slaves revolted at any point between 1860 and 1865, the war would have come to screeching halt. But they did not. Yet in what museum will you hear the story of how Southern blacks sustained the home front of the South during the war?

Today's stories in museums are more about victimization than they are about life and relationships, and the whole South, black and white, working together.

While some privately owned museums could be considered part of the Southern movement, only a keen inspection with a vigilant eye could discern that. I remember personal disgust when visiting Stonewall Jackson's home in Lexington, Virginia, to hear an employee authoritatively spew Yankee history while standing in the home of Ole Jack. My heart broke knowing how many ears this poison had infected.

There are few known national figures who speak for the Southern point of view. Shelby Foote, a wonderful author of the great conflict may be the last Douglas Southall Freeman-type storyteller for the South. These two men wrote the war from a perspective which gave the Southern point of view legitimacy and for a long time, almost the entire second half of the twentieth century, their interpretations of history had great effect on professors and teachers all across the nation. (I have read more than twenty-five thousand pages of history of this era, and no modern historians come close to these two in their ability to relate the Southern perspective of the era and the war Only the words of Davis, Lee and other first person accounts, are superior to these two men in telling the story.)

Dr. Thomas DiLorenzo of Loyola College in Maryland may not be a part of the Southern movement, but his work has articulated the Southern view of democracy as no other in modern times. In an article titled "The Great Centralizer: Abraham Lincoln and the War between the States," Dr. DiLorenzo follows up on a theme about President Lincoln developed in his book. DiLorenzo talks at length about how Lincoln undid the Republic to save the Union. For the modern Southern movement, his theme is central to its existence.

Another place you don't see the South as it once was is in the Christian churches of the South. Here should be fertile ground for the South of old. In the Preamble of the Confederate Constitution, Southerners called on God for His wisdom and protection. Christianity was a large part of the South and is still. But the connection between the tattered Confederate gray and the Cross is no longer there. Few pastors of the South have read *Christ in the Camp*, the story of Christian revivals in the Southern armies. And there seems a division or distance between the Southern movement and the great majority of churches in the South.

www.independent.org/pdf/tir/tir_03_2_dilorenzo.pdf

Political elements within the movement

There are political elements within the Southern movement. One of them, the Southern National Congress, www.southernnationalcongress.org, has been active for about five years. This group's purpose is to formulate and articulate a Southern viewpoint which can echo in the halls of Congress. The group meets annually to discuss issues and address resolutions brought to the Congress by delegates from all the Southern states. Many of the attendees are writers and thinkers of different disciplines struggling with the America of today.

The Southern National Congress is representative of the people of the South, its views more populist in nature. The Convent of the Congress www.southernnationalcongress.org southernnationalcovenant.shtml is fairly specific in its condemnation of present US policies and its expression of the concept of a Southern nation.

Mark Thomey has been a member of the League of the South and also the Sons of Confederate Veterans. He is the present chair of the Southern National Congress. Coming from Louisiana, Mark Thomey is an unreconstructed Southerner. "There have always been two America's, one Yankee and one Southern." Thomey talks a lot about secession and about a Southern nation. He believes there is very much a subdued Southern nation. Thomey believes many Southerners have been hobbled by Yankee occupation and brainwashing.

Mark said, "Yes, there is a Southern movement, among the people of the South, something is really wrong, and we have to fix it. Southerners believe we are not the same as the rest of America. But this feeling is deep inside and has been covered over. There is a constant internal struggle."

"The movement is those of us who have finally decided to look at the US regime for what it really is. Evil people are bent on our destruction as a people. The Southern National Congress is the tip of the spear. Other organizations are lagging behind in seeing a modern Southern nation."

Mark Thomey saw recently that a poll indicated as many as one in five people support the idea of secession as a political alternative in today's world. The SNC is shifting gears so as to try to become an umbrella organization for the movement. "Our first couple of years we were a debating society, but now we are trying to set ourselves up as a more legitimate political alternative to what presently exists."

Chairman Thomey announced, "The SNC is planning to put together an international conference on secession."

It is their hope that as Americans, descendants of men who separated themselves from an oppressive monarchy and, as the heirs to Southern secession, they will be able to help Americans understand the position of foreign peoples who wish only for independence and liberty.

In addition, the SNC has set a course for its delegates to engage state legislatures in legislation endorsed by the SNC. This is a tremendous first step toward real political activity on behalf of Southern movement. It begins the process of practicing citizenship and learning how to influence government policy.

Another political group, the League of the South, is more concerned with the principle of secession. Formed in June of 1994, the League's stated purpose is to organize the people of the South to pursue an independent nation. However, the League clearly states it does not seek armed revolution, but rather a peaceful, legal means of secession.

The League does believe in the absolute connection between the Southern culture and Christianity. They state: "As an organization we do recognize the legacy of Christianity and

the universal sovereignty of the triune God. Most League members are Christians and we base our movement on Christian principles. Trinitarian Christianity cannot be separated or removed from Southern society or culture without both ceasing to be Southern."
http://dixienet.org/rights/index.shtml

Observation
For the most part, each element or organization within the Southern movement operates without cooperation or even contact with the others. And from my viewpoint, this inability to cooperate epitomizes the Southern failure in the war for their independence, the present plague of combat ineffectiveness in both the Culture War and the political course the United States has taken.

While individuals across the South share many hopes, aspirations and values, fissures and firebreaks have been created by leaders in some of the Southern heritage organizations to prevent the formation of political efforts on behalf of the South and its culture. Censorship is used to keep the movement divided. The Internet has helped to challenge this censorship, but it has not eliminated it. Leaders decide what they want their people to hear about and what they don't. They then censor messages based on those calls.

For some who think about the internal dynamics of the Southern movement, they see censorship as a question of ego and control. But I think the overt efforts to limit communications, and thus cooperation between the various elements within the Southern movement, has a more devious objective — to limit the combat effectiveness of all Southern movement organizations in the Culture War.

The Confederate War College
Some leaders in the South are interested in facilitating communications between the organizations. Some leaders want free speech and the free exchange of ideas. The Confederate War College will be a new addition to the Southern movement. Privately operated, this site will publish articles submitted from whomever. Controversial ideas will be encouraged. The idea is to strengthen the South and expand the cooperation of the different elements. We hope to live by the very virtues of Southerners like Thomas Jefferson and George Washington.

Is there a Southern movement?
Regretfully, I must conclude that there is not. A movement, in political terms, would have a purpose, direction and degree of unity not present in the disparate groups we have identified. The Southern National Congress does express political ambitions, but it has not grown and has not connected with other elements within the movement.

The heritage organizations, specifically the Sons of Confederate Veterans, are impotent in terms of political power. Despite their membership size and century-old organization, they are combat ineffective in the Culture War. The SCV does not lobby Congress or the state legislatures for their *Cause*. They do not create a legislative agenda as other similar type organizations do. And efforts to create political action committees (PACs) floundered because of a lack of persistence reflecting a lack of interest at the leadership levels.

In part, the South is dying because her *guardians* are not organized to defend her.

Commercially, the South has failed to take advantage of the thousands of historic sites located there. Gettysburg, a small town in southern Pennsylvania, annually nets more than 300 million dollars in tourist revenue, employing more than 6,000 persons. In the South many political leaders/bureaucrats have gone to great lengths not to preserve Southern battlefields or promote Southern culture as a tourist attraction. The Civil War may well be the most-read American history, creating the sale of hundreds of millions of dollars of books, but Southern investors have not seen fit to take advantage of a prepared market to develop the historical properties which would enshrine Southern culture.

Agriculture is still a large part of the South's economy, but growing cities and a densely populated coastline have overwhelmed traditional Southern views of life. Christianity still survives in much of the South, but more so in the rural areas where there is less population.

It may be more accurate to say that there is a Southern tradition. This tradition shows itself at fairs and parades and cemeteries. You can hear the tradition on the Internet from time to time. But the tradition is not reflective of the tens of millions of Americans whose roots go back to Dixie. Listen carefully, you may be hearing its dying breaths.

Is there a Southern movement? Part II

Things are heating up in the South and much more could be written about the South.

As disputes across Virginia between authorities and Southern patriots unfold, I decided to do a follow-up article on the Southern movement.

In Part II we will focus more on people who are active in fighting the political correctness cancer which has infested much of the South's institutions and heritage organizations. And, we will we talk with Dr. Hill, president of the League of the South.

The Flaggers in Richmond

Has the South found its own version of Sarah Palin? I could not help but think that as I talked with Susan Hathaway in a late night telephone interview for this article.

Mrs. Hathaway started her protest of the Virginia Museum of Fine Arts twenty-nine weeks ago. Her initial flagging efforts were to get the Museum to reverse its policy regarding the removal of the Confederate Colors at the Confederate Chapel. In the beginning there was just one lone flagger, herself. She said that within three weeks three people were gathering for the protest. And now twenty-nine weeks later she normally has fifteen Flaggers to stand with her one day a week from 3 p.m. to dusk. "The days are getting longer as dusk moves later and later," she kidded as she told me about her activities that day.

These flaggers, mothers, grandfathers, children sometimes, are sure dangerous folks. The Museum of the Confederacy lays on extra security when they know the flaggers will be around. So Susan and the other leaders switch the days, just to give the museum a little heartburn. "The longer this goes on, the more the Museum tries to intimidate us with extra security and tougher restrictions on where we can walk." said Susan.

The flaggers are combining their protests for the flying of a flag at the Chapel and protesting the Museum of the Confederacy, which is only a short distance away.

When asked about the media coverage, Susan said that generally the news coverage has been pretty fair, "50 – 50," especially the television coverage. "You have to understand, we are in the museum district of Richmond, which is very liberal. There are Obama stickers everywhere. But we do meet people who are supportive of our efforts and the media has been better than I thought it would be."

When a news story about the Museum ran without any coverage of the flaggers, Susan knew to pick up the phone and give the reporter a call. That call resulted in a second article, one she believes was favorable to the flaggers' goal.

Susan gives a lot credit to Billy Bearden of Georgia and Grayson Jennings of Richmond. "Those two guys have been real advisers to our efforts. They know how to do things like we are attempting." Billy Bearden had been active in the fights about the Georgia state flag almost twenty years ago.

The flaggers have not just been protestors in the streets. Mrs. Hathaway reports they have been active at committee meetings at the state legislature. She believes her group's activities helped kill three different bills while they were still in committee. One bill was going to change President's Day in Virginia to Lincoln's Day. Another bill was going to create a Slavery Commission, which translates to establishing a platform to discuss reparations.

Though these are activities the Sons of Confederate Veterans (SCV) and United Daughters of the Confederacy should be active in, it seems this *ad hoc* group of Southern patriots is doing more with much less to meet General Lee's Charge.

But Susan speaks very highly of Michael Givens, commander of the Sons of Confederate Veterans. "I have been very impressed with Michael," Susan said. "He is trying to coordinate activities between the large heritage groups." Susan was full of kind compliments for Commander Givens.

Givens had issued a letter to the SCV general membership after the SCV national board of directors issued a resolution calling for a boycott of the Appomattox grand opening March 31.

While Susan was not willing to divulge future planning for operations, she did say they were working on a couple things. "I would love to see these kinds of activity spread spontaneously across the South," Susan wished quietly as we ended our call. Her prayers are not hers alone, as patriots all across the South have been disappointed with the lack of action by the heritage organizations.

The Southern Nationalist Network (SNN)

At 6,500 hits per week, Michael Cushman's SNN will get more than three hundred thousand hits per year! And Cushman's site is different from many other Southern websites in that he provides both written stories and podcasts. The podcasts feature audio interviews with Southern patriots concerning a wide variety of issues. This site is a reliable source of news concerning the Southern nationalist movement.

Michael Cushman, 35 years old, knows his subject matter. He has a bachelor's degree in history from the University of South Carolina at Aiken, but he insists he learned much more after he graduated, than while he was in class. Michael was formerly a member of the Sons of Confederate Veterans, but like so many other former SCV members, Michael became disillusioned by the *granny* attitudes prevalent in so much of the organization. And through our discussion — interview, I came to have great respect for Michael's insights.

Michael's first experience with the SCV was when troubles sprang up in Aiken, South Carolina. There was a movement afoot to rename Wade Hampton Avenue to Martin Luther King Avenue. The local SCV camp sprang into action to prevent this action by the city council. But Michael was disappointed that the camp did not use the money it had collected for the fight nor the momentum the camp had gained in its successful fight to do more.

Aiken is a very wealthy town, "almost all Yankees. Pretty much all of the Southerners have been pushed out. Mostly wealthy Yankees now." Said Michael. "The SCV has a big camp and they do a lot, but they pledge to the US Flag. I have always been more radical than the SCV. The SCV maintains memorials and they run the Battle of Aiken."

Michael decided to use his efforts for a more aggressive campaign; the result is his work on the Internet. He believes there is still "a nation, an ethnic group and a culture" which exists within the modern South.

Michael said, "Secession is the fundamental right, which is the only real meaningful check on a centralized government." I could hear Donnie Kennedy in Michael's words.

Many in the Southern movement believe what Michael said next: "The US Empire is on the way out. If we can preserve our national identity and prevent an amalgamation and assimilation within a larger group, we may still persevere in creating a free South."

Michael introduced a new observation I had not heard before: "There is a huge generational schism between old Southerners and the new South; younger Southerners are not as assimilated into the US." Michael believes many younger people see the decline and collapse of America more readily than older people. He says these younger people have a grasp of the original intent of the Founding Fathers of the United States.

The Southern Nationalist Network is about 18 months old, and is an upgrade from Michael's first website, the Southern Liberation Media News. Michael does not have advertising on his site, but he does accept donations to help offset the cost of running a news network. Michael said this is not a money-making venture.

In closing our talk, Michael made a statement which seems to echo across all the people I talk to within the Southern movement: "A Southerner will always know another Southerner."

In the first article I did mention the League of the South. But the information provided was from their website and secondary interviews. This time I went straight to the man who has been the president of the League for its 18 years of existence, Dr. Michael Hill.

The League of the South
Dr. Hill earned his Ph.D. in history at the University of Alabama. Dr. Hill was cordial and frank in our discussion. He explained the League formed in Tuscaloosa, Alabama, in June of 1994 in response to actions against the South, and because the Sons of Confederate Veterans and other heritage organizations were not organized for the purpose Dr. Hill and others had in mind.

The purpose of the League: "The League of the South is a Southern nationalist organization whose ultimate goal is a free and independent Southern republic. To reach this goal, we intend to create the climate for a free South among our people by the 1) delimitation of the American Empire at every opportunity; 2) by proving our willingness to be servant-leaders to the Southern people; and 3) by making The League of the South a strong, viable organization that will lead us to Southern independence."

Simply stated, the goal of the League is: "To advance the cultural, social, economic, and political well-being and independence of the Southern people by all honorable means."

On its home page the League rejects the notion that it is a revolutionary outfit intending to overthrow the US government. The League also rejects racism . ..very important since any new Southern nation would have a strong African-American and Mexican influence.

Presently, the League has between four and six thousand members. Most of the members reside in the South, but there are sizable memberships in New York and California.

Dr. Hill explained: "We believe that there is still an Anglo-Celtic core in the South (western Christendom) culturally close enough to be common." He went on to say the cultural homogenization of the American people is eroding the Southern culture and many in the South have been influenced by Yankee occupation of the South and Reconstructionist history. What occupation could not do, nationalized television and radio are doing.

I asked Dr. Hill if he had seen an increase in membership as a result of the Sesquicentennial and he replied, "No." But he said there were two spikes in membership recently. The first occurred when President Bush conducted the first bailout; the second after the election of President Barack Obama.

The League is not a democratic organization. Leaders are selected from the top. The League has a national office, state chapters and local chapters. Authority is generously delegated down through the states to the local chapters. I sensed there was a goal to get a chapter in every county in the South.

While the League is not a heritage organization and does not organize or work on heritage defense issues like the battles occurring in Richmond, Appomattox and Lexington, many members of the League work with other Southern patriots on these type of issues.

Dr. Hill said the Southern National Congress came into existence in large part because the leadership of the League felt there needed to be a political voice for the South. However, Dr. Hill insisted the League and the Congress are two separate organizations, each operating independently of the other. "More than half the delegates who attend the annual Congress meetings are members of the League," Hill said.

Dr. Hill said the majority of the work being done by the League is organizational. Much effort is being expended in organizing local chapters across the South and establishing an internal communications system which could withstand disruption caused by a natural or political emergency. Dr. Hill believes the United States is in a state of decline and could actually cease to exist as a result of a number of ongoing trends. If it does, he says he wants the League to be prepared for such an eventuality.

The Southern Partisan Reader

Tim Manning is a prolific writer and activist in the South. His website, the Southern Partisan Reader, is a warehouse of essays concerning the South. Tim is published continually through Southern Heritage News and Views. Among other activities, Tim is responsible for the educational material associated with the Stephen D. Lee Institute, an educational arm of the Sons of Confederate Veterans.

Tim is a very well-read thinker who believes "The melting pot is a concept of social conditioning intended to create a cultural flavor which began at the end of the 19th century. This new influence was not American, Southern or Christian. There is no conservative movement in America any more …" It was not just the Southern states who were reconstructed.

When asked if there is a Southern movement, Tim replied: "Asking it in the singular? No. Are there Southern movements? Yes. A lot of the different movements are becoming more aware of that there is a general consensus of opinion and thought." But Tim acknowledges that much of what the South was is gone. "The South today is not philosophically different from the rest of the nation." However, elements are distinctively different from the rest of the country in many vital respects, especially among more devout Christians, but still it is very reconstructed.

When you talk to Tim about his life experience and his opinions of present-day America you hear a kind of disappointment widespread amongst many men who consider themselves Southern: "We have not found that the people of this nation were interested in the view of the Founders." Tim's view touched a nerve with me as I believe the exercise of citizenship within our nation has collapsed in most Americans to a very a small materially centered attitude. What we each receive from government seems to be at the essence of our individual citizenship, and we have ignored or rejected the legacy of liberty passed down to us.

One historic reality, whitewashed out of the politically correct version of the causes for secession that the South of 1860, was the Southern belief that it was holding true to the original Constitution. The North and Abe Lincoln sought a more powerful central government to use political power to assist commercial activity and shape the nation. The South hoped to keep central government at arm's length on most domestic issues and allow commerce to occur unfettered. For the South, if there was to be molding of commerce, it should occur in the states allowing the sovereignty of the states to be preserved.

Manning is more open to the idea that the South is not ethnically what it once was. He said: "The South is not a monolithic culture and never has been for any significant period of time." But Manning also expresses a widespread disappointment that regionalism on television has vanished, and that the centralized control of national television is quickly dissipating the Southern identity. "We would like to see the qualities of the South aired in the modern media."

When asked about the Southern National Congress, Manning said they formed "because they see the US as disintegrating." This reflects a theme espoused by Virginian Patrick Buchanan in many of his books.

While Manning readily admits to the influx of Mexican and Yankee settlers in large parts of the South, he asserts, "A lot of people in the South consider themselves as much a unique group as any other nationality. There are a group of people in the South who are distinct. When our speakers speak to groups, you can see lights come on as they recognize that they do feel like the speaker is saying."

When I made the comment that many people in the South, including some in the Sons of Confederate Veterans, are ashamed of being from the South, Tim replied; "I believe your observation is a great one. This is the natural result of years of the indoctrination conditioning that we call 'reconstruction' or 'yankeefication.'"

Living in North Carolina, Tim Manning is on one of the front lines of the evolving South. The high-tech triangle which has risen in central Carolina brought with it about 45,000 higher income high-tech workers (most from outside Carolina) who could be the swing vote in that state, which will decide its choice on election day.

On the movement

Manning's comment that there are many movements in the South appears to be the most accurate. There is no revolutionary movement that I can find. There is no one who wants to overthrow the government or force secession.

The folks most obvious in the Confederate uniforms, the reenactors and the Sons of Confederate Veterans, are probably the least concerned with any future South. Their view is backward. They seem focused on the history. While the *Charge* of the Sons of Confederate Veterans is in the present tense, "vindicate the Cause," a large number of them do not see "vindicate" for its definition in the dictionary. They do not see justification of the *Cause* for its political ramifications. And many like Waite Rawls at the Museum of the Confederacy are more comfortable in allowing the dust of history to bury the patriotic zeal that was the South.

One group missing from this article is African-Americans. They are an integral part of the future of the South. They have been an integral part of the South from its earliest moments. During the War for Southern Independence, it was the African-American community which did not revolt but remained loyal to the South, who made the plantations work, and were part of the home front infrastructure for the war. And many blacks fought for the South as freedman and slave. Their contributions have been sorely under reported because it is inconvenient history. But in any new South, black Southerners would be essential.

Some in the Southern movement believe America is collapsing across a broad front morally, financially, culturally and with respect to its origination. A common thread I have found, even when not openly articulated, is that "we are waiting." We are waiting for the day when without us, and not because of us, chaos will erupt. At that point, new political arrangements will have to be made and then the South may reemerge as a nation.

How does the South reclaim its legacy?

Introduction

This article is intended for all Americans, and those in the South who see the ongoing attack on American history, heritage, culture, exceptionalism, and nationalism as a coordinated multi-pronged effort to neuter the United States of America. I submit the attack on the South, since the late 1960s, is the point of the spear being driven into the very heart of the United States.

It is an assumption of this essay that the South is a region within the United States unique in it's own "sub-national identity," way of life, history, and view of the Constitution. The South was always more than the single issue (slavery) most associated with the region. The South's reputation as the Bible Belt is perhaps the single most important definer. Christianity is at the core of its culture, and the South was instrumental in its contribution to America's political systems. While this author recognizes that each geographic region within America has degrees of culture, history, pride and politics, it is my assertion the South, with its Confederate Battle Flag and regional anthem of *Dixie*, stands alone. The American South is world recognized through its revered symbols.

It is the premise of this essay that the attack on the South by the secular social engineers is an important aspect of their larger attack on the United States because of the innate loyalty of Southerners to their region. The goal of these engineers is to rearrange America so as to make it an extension of the Euro Union, and a broken state eager for assimilation into a global government.[1] Therefore, the preservation and perpetuity of *Southern Legacy* is vital to the national interest of the United States.

To save the legacy of the South is essentially a political activity. This activity is not inher-

---

[1]Rush Limbaugh just weeks before this article was written spoke several times over a series of days about the attack on the South by the main stream media.

ently partisan (Democrat or Republican), though for the moment the first steps towards a revival of the South must be focused on the Republican Party, or its conservative replacement should the GOP collapse.

In this book, *Southern Fried Ramblings with Grits and all the Fixins* I provide a broad survey of the contemporary Southern movement, the issues, the different people, groups and organizations involved and whether their activities are successful in growing their membership. But one thing is evident, the various groups do not coordinate their efforts, nor is there a long range plan for restoring a unified Southern presence in America.

Before we talk about how to organize a revival of the Southern legacy, I should like to share my thoughts on why, when, how and where the glory and cultural heart of the South became a target of the present day ruling elite, an elite which is neither solely Yankee, nor solely American. I am sure you will easily recognize everything discussed in the next paragraphs, but possibly you never connected them all to see the broader picture. I assert our opponents, the people behind the assassination of the South do see the bigger picture, and do have an objective even larger than the great Southland. Their real target is the United States.

I believe the attack on the South began sometime after the 100th anniversary of the War for Southern Independence in the years 1961-1965. Though just a child at that time, I can remember many things across America honoring both the war and the South. At that time, television, radio and print media were still regionalized. National broadcasting was still in its infancy, and had not as yet attempted to erase regional viewpoints for one consolidated eastern establishment *theology*.

In movies, whether it be *Sgt. York*, or *Gone with the Wind* or Disney's *Song of the South*, the great Southern traditions of faith, family and patriotism were evident. The relationship between white and black in the South was portrayed more as a united, friendly, even loving relationship. Probably much more as it really was, than is portrayed now. (I am not defending slavery, I myself condemn it as sin. Still I know from my grandmother that slaves were treated as family in the hills in west central North Carolina, and possibly most of the rest of the South.) Andy Griffith had no trouble including humorous references to the war, and the South in his popular, long running national television show.

But with the late sixties and seventies the America of old was invaded by a horde, seemingly coordinated by a central evil which sees the Constitution and this nation for what it was intended, a place for Christ to flourish. Their target is the destruction of the America founded in 1776. When you look at the arsenal of their victories it is difficult to come up with any other conclusion;

    a. The legal slaughter of 55 million innocents as a result of a tyrannical decision by the Supreme Court. The supposed guardian of the Constitution struck at the "right to life" and set a standard, a flag flying marking the arrival of Satan.

    b. The massive use of illegal drugs by a large percentage of the American population, operating an underground commercial operation which dwarfs all but the largest of legal American business.

 c. The gutting of the FCC and the downward moral spiral of entertainment across the spectrum, from Hannity's bold embrace of profanity to the garbage stories of destroyed human lives and spirit which fill our living rooms in the evening.
 d. The use of lotteries and other forms of gambling to fund government, and the infestation of casinos on the lands of America's first people.
 e. The chasing of God from our public schools and the continuous attack on the Church. Now the First Amendment is clearly an objective where the central government attempts to force the church to abide, to bend their knee to Caesar.
 f. The social ills of homosexuality, divorce, broken families, the confusion of the roles of man and woman, and the wrong-headed ideas of tolerance and diversity.
 g. The attack on the concept of States' Rights and the diminution of the sovereignty of the creators of the Union, both states and individual citizen.
 h. The trashing of the concept of national patriotism (begun with the Vietnam War antiwar crowd, but extended throughout the society today.) so that a commercial concept of globalization could then remove the idea of the nation-state, and instead look for a one world government!
 i. The replacement of the concepts of work, savings, patience, and building a life with God, one brick at a time to credit, debt, a fast food mentality on self-gratification and an anything goes morality.

All of these things are occurring throughout the United States, so where does the Southern legacy fit in?

Simple, all of those things are ***anti-Southern***. When one reads the Confederate Constitution, the bedrock of Southern political thinking, we find a document which begins with a recognition of God in the Preamble, and a national aspiration to be His, to seek His guidance, and His protection. From the very first, the Southern nation extended but more boldly proclaimed one of the foundational underpinnings of the creation of the United States, the role of God in governing the place![2]

OK, so how did the South become the target?

From here on we will go somewhere you may not want to go. At least many connected to the modern Southern movement in the heritage organizations have resisted. From here we go to the arena of politics!

Politics — Economy — Cultural Identity

The campaign the South needs to engage in occurs on three fronts, politics, economics, and cultural identity.

In the 1960s the South was the anchor of the Democrat party. It was a solid block. As solidly Democrat then as New York, Massachusetts and California are today. And the South was

---

[2] To really understand the founding of the United States I strongly recommend *Forged in Faith, The Christian Life and Character of the Civil Institutions of the United States*, and Chapter 5, *The South Was Right!*

still the South. If you went to an Old Miss game, or for that matter a Friday night high school football game you were likely to hear *Dixie* as a fight song, after you prayed. If you went to a NASCAR event you would see the Confederate Battle Flag waving not just from the stands, but actually painted on the cars that raced around the track. Many, if not most Southern political leaders had some affiliation with their local Sons of Confederate Veterans.

In many respects the defiance of the South was then unreconstructed. Some of what went on in the South, and in the North, the racism, was an evil of Satan. But most of what the South was, was good. It was family, God, state. Air conditioning had only been recently invented back then, and the Yankees had not come in their second wave of invasion yet.

But they were about to. And this time their weapon would not be the bayonet but money.

Money, Yankee money and foreign money would change the South, alter its cultural center of gravity. It would take advantage of a Tory[3] element which had existed even in the heat and passion of secession. These Tories had never been a part of the South spiritually and in modern times they are ashamed of Southern history and Southern culture. They are the fifth column within the South. In the heritage organizations they are called *grannies*, the men and women who wear uniforms and period dressed but shutter whenever anyone suggests a more aggressive stance towards the promotion of the South. They see their "vindication of the Cause" in small, quaint social events of no consequence, and do all they can to block the formation of modern Southern legions prepared to enter the fray of modern American politics with an objective of reasserting the Southern legacy. They warn "we are prevented...."

I would assert that many of these grannies are actually modern liberals whose personal inclinations are driven by causes outside those of the South. They could be government workers, union members, atheists, Libertarians or others who place their personal agenda above the retaking of the South. They assert they are "proud of their heritage" but their love for the old South ends there. They don't want to bring it back. They like America and the South as it is, and as it is evolving, ever leftward and ever more agnostic.

So within the very ranks of the Southern movement is the first line defense against a revival of the South, and a revival of America. (While many in the Southern movement cannot see the two together, I do. And because I accept secession as American, I can accept a state's right to secede. In fact I see that right as essential to maintaining the original checks and balances within the Constitution itself.)

Back to the Democrat Party. When the liberals in the '70s and beyond took over the party and consolidated their position, they began to embrace political concepts like socialism which were anathema to the South. For a time, the South stayed Democrat despite these moves because of their justified hatred of the other party. Reconstruction left a bitter taste which was not easily forgotten. But in 1980 a man came along who had a bottle of mouthwash, Ronald

---

[3] In central and western North Carolina the term Tory was applied to Yankee sympathizers at the time of the war.

Reagan. And from that time, until recently, the South has been solidly Republican. Why? Because the South is conservative, and the Republicans had demonstrated (at least for a while) they were significantly more conservative.

But the Republicans, though they needed the South for its Senators, and its electoral votes had long had its own ruling elite. Dominated by the mid-west and northeast, Republicans were more conservative solely because of commercial reasons, and the threat of the Soviet Union. They made accommodations to the South because they needed them. However, with the fall of the Soviet Union, much changed.

Today we see the Republicans as narrowly defending some of their commercial interests to the exclusion of all else. But a lot of the commercial interests are now focused on foreign markets and foreign production. Asia is seen as the next bonanza for profits.[4] And corporations which during the Cold War had waved the flag, now have put the United States flag in the closet. While Main Street is still in America, Wall Street is everywhere but.

The Republicans have replaced God, with their God, commerce. Anything which hinders commerce, including God, borders, morality, patriotism, standards, nationalism are all to demeaned and eradicated.

For the Southerner this creates a real question. How do we forward our colors in the arena of politics?

Actually, there is a great opportunity here. Neither party, at their core, is pro-Southern, or pro any values which are Southern. So that makes the choices a tactical one, depending on who needs our votes the most. Whoever will do the most to forward our cause deserves consideration.

We who want a pro-South agenda must do what other special interests do. We must place our *Cause* above other priorities in our lives. Politics is about choices and priorities. I believe that for grannies and others who seemingly sabotage Southern initiatives, their motives are certain, their purpose to stall the South.

But at the moment we are treading on ground forbidden to heritage organizations. Let's move towards the politics which is fertile ground for the *Cause*. That fertile ground is the governing of America, your state, county, board of education, etc.

The Politics of Governance

Where the South, and its guardians have been completely inept is creating an agenda to take to the government to implement. The Southern movement has been passive — laying on the porch like a lazy hound dog, barking only after some coyote has snatched Briar Rabbit. There has been absolutely no initiative, or offensive campaign to re-assert the Southern legacy.

Were you to attend a Veterans' organization (VFW, Legion, Vietnam Vets, Amvets, etc.) national convention you would find that a great deal of time is spent on creating a legislative

---

[4]Important to note here that many scholars, etc. in the world of military affairs believe the United States is re-orienting its military focus to the Pacific, despite the promised Obama reductions.

agenda for the organization. Tens, if not more than hundred, resolutions will be addressed at the various veterans' conventions concerning everything from defense and foreign policy issues, to veterans' programs, budgeting, pay and benefits, etc. Like heritage organizations, the veterans are prohibited from any activity which aids in the actual election of favored candidates. However they work hard to influence government policy no matter who is in office!

And this is where the South has been dismally inept.

A real reason for the failure is apathy. Yes apathy. Most Americans pay very little attention to the work of governing the nation, or expend their own resources and time to participate. This apathy is as prevalent in the Southern movement as it is anywhere else in society,

Part of this is caused by the Southern tradition of wanting to ignore government as much as possible. There is a Libertarian strain in *Southernness*, one which abhors government. In Texas it is almost sacred. Government is like the small pox, you don't want it.

But the real danger in this kind of thinking is that Yankees, and other sorts, will take advantage of the vacuum created by Southern absence, and take everything government can give them (which means Southern monies collected in taxes). Then they will cry about what they did not get. Their agenda is endless. The have an appetite which cannot be quenched, as is evidenced by a 16 trillion dollar debt.

Southern heritage organizations have failed completely in this duty. There is no legislative agenda, no legislative directors at the federal and state levels. There are no liaison officers from camps and chapters to local government, and state and federal officials. (Something all veterans' organizations do.)

While the Southern agenda need not be overly expensive, it does need to have money connected to it to make it real. Money is value and in politics it is one of the currencies of deals and power.

For the South and promotion of the South dollars could be connected to:

    a. Confederate cemeteries (like the ones in Richmond) which should have decent headstones promised by the Veterans Administration but never coming.

    b. Funding for Confederate and Southern museums, festivals, cultural events which promote not only the old South, but the present one.

    c. Block grants to states to provide domestic services currently administered at the federal level, but which should be conducted at the state level. These grants should be reduced through time, allowing the states to fund them completely.

    d. Removal of the Department of Education at the federal level, and ending all subsidies for public education by the federal government. (Possibly the greatest threat to individual freedom and the concept of the Republic is the US Department of Education)

    e. Funding for Confederate, pro-South historical interpretations at federal and or state parks dedicated to the War for Southern Independence.

    f. Seeing inclusion of the Southern point of view in the historical interpretation of the antebellum years, secession and the invasion by the Union.

Some in the Southern movement would point to lawsuits as their favored method of interacting with government. I submit that this form of interaction is:

    a. Ineffective and costly, siphoning off resources from other more worthwhile publicity, recruiting, marketing and educational activities.

    b. Severely restricts the chance to engage the membership.

    c. Removes an opportunity for recruiting.

    d. Plays the game most likely to end up in the status quo's favor, in part because a small elite leadership decides what deals to cut, and what actions to prevent within its own organization to forward the cause. (Repeated failure demonstrates either a conspiracy within the leadership, or just as bad exceptionally poor judgment.)

The point of this portion of the paper is to illustrate that there are means to participate in the political arena. In Virginia and Georgia groups calling themselves Flaggers are investing time in public protest on behalf of the South. Their devotion, self-commitment, tireless work are to be commended and supported. But left to only this tactic I am afraid progress will be very slow, if at all.

In politics, as in war, there are arsenals of weapons with different purposes and uses, all to be used to attain the objective. Public protest, rallies are one form, or one weapon in the arsenal. But, like infantry, if unsupported by artillery, air cover, naval bombardment, tanks, helicopters, missiles, etc., the infantry can easily be contained and defeated by a force with just one more asset, one more weapon not committed to the infantry.

A campaign to reclaim the Southern legacy must include all aspects of political operations; fund raising, marketing, polling, media messaging, rallies, communications, base building, etc.

It would be easiest to accomplish this within existing heritage organizations. They have the chain of command, the membership, the structure. But alas, that fifth column has already infested and paralyzed these organizations.

So if there is to be a revival of the South, it seems that there must be a new organization created with one purpose; to affect a Southern agenda. Now the Southern National Congress has claimed this ground. The Congress is only a few years old.

Their efforts to date are a promotion of peculiar non-starter causes which have no real basis in the South, or today's Southerners. They make no effort to represent the South, to determine what the people of the South actually think, but instead remain isolated as a small group with nothing else to do. In existence for a few years, I have yet to hear of public forums, nor have I seen any effort to solicit the real thoughts of the majority of the people of the greater South. No political party has started. Worse, they deal in unreality instead of the political reality of today.

For the South to live, to revive, a realistic assessment of today's people and views is essential. Certainly there are Southerners who revere the original South, but they are few. Even native born, generations here Southerners do not know the true history and political values of the South.

Economics as an effective political influence

If you remember earlier in the paper we talked about NASCAR. Remember the Confederate flag proudly waving. Not anymore. When the big money came to NASCAR the monied people made the removal of the flag non-negotiable. And throughout the universities in the South the same has happened.

It's time for Southerners to reverse that. How?

If a cause comes to you for money, tell them you want some indication they are proud of their Southern roots. If they won't, then refuse to donate. Make it known why, make it known you want a Southern presence, or you will look elsewhere to contribute.

If it comes to purchasing as a consumer, don't buy from those who attack the South or Christianity. Boycott; it doesn't have to be loud, it just has to be long and growing to be effective. And you need to talk to your family and friends about it. At the same time, those businesses which are pro-Southern deserve support. You need to buy from them, and you need to tell them why.

If one town is supportive of the *Cause* and another not; go to the one which is supportive and purchase from them. Tell them why. On the way home, go to the town which is not supportive, take your receipt into the equivalent store, hand it to them and tell them why your money went somewhere else.

Money has to flow towards the South, not just geographically, but towards the South we want to revive if it is to happen. Money has momentum. It may start as a small trickle towards the *Cause*, but as more and more people hear and make the same consumer decisions, the trickle can become a roaring tide.

While we may not like the power of money to influence reality, the fact is that if we don't accept its role and turn it to our own ends we shall forever fail to reach our goal. If you want a Southern legacy it will take money to create it, sustain it, and protect it.

In the 1970s and 1980s entertainment dollars flowed towards musical groups like Alabama, the Allman Brothers and many others.

Cultural Identity

At first glance, for some, *Cultural Identity* may seem obvious, or a no brainer. I would contend it may be the most difficult part of reclaiming the Southern legacy.

In 1860 the South might easily claim to be more diverse in cultural identity than the North. The South not only had most of the same Euro migration sects, but obviously had a multi-sect slave class, plus a somewhat integrated Indian element (like the Cherokees in North Carolina, and the Six Nations of present day Oklahoma) but also had the mixture of French-Spanish Cajuns, and the Mexicans of Texas. All of these peoples were a part of the South and all contributed to the *Cause*.

Divisions between white and black appear to have been exacerbated intentionally in the late 50s-60s to the present. Racism exists, though it is below the surface.

Yet, the whole South fought the Union. Slaves did not revolt during the war. Had three million slaves, or even a relatively small percentage of them, revolted during the war it could have changed the course of the war and brought it to a much quicker conclusion.

But the opposite occurred. The slaves, for the most part, remained loyal and even participated at the front in the armies.

So if this element of history were to be revealed it might work to heal some of today's wounds and possibly change attitudes. But that is not the only challenge for the new South. Like the rest of America, millions of illegal immigrants have settled in the South. And then of course, there are large numbers of Yankee immigrants who bring with them a Yankee slant.

For there to be a real revival and rebirth of the South, as a region, accommodations would have to be made to include and assimilate different cultures. If this issue is not addressed and considered, the new South would continue the problems created by America's century's old hodgepodge immigration policy. At its core, the South would still retain its Christian Anglo-Celtic traditions though somewhat diminished by the absorption and inclusion of so many other cultures. Some in the Southern movement have real problems with this reality.

In the antebellum era the South was strong because of the living and working relationships of its various peoples. Somehow this *Southern unity* must be recreated through equality and not submission.

Summation

As you can see from this brief and incomplete presentation, there will be a lot of work to revive a Southern legacy, a modern version. Looking at it, it seems so daunting, so large that no one could possible achieve it in a hundred years. And yet, as Christians we know the power of our God, and that all happens in His time. So it is possible, and it can happen faster than we could ever imagine if it be His will and His time.

The question is will you pray on this? Will you consider it? Will you talk to others about it?

What happened in Memphis is neither a beginning or an end. If we do nothing these won't be the last parks renamed, or the last time the South will endure embarrassment. And if we do determine to commence a real campaign and do the work in the political arena it still will be decades before things may change.

I have done what I have been given to do.

◠ Section IV ◠

Scotland and Secession

Secession is not unique to America!

Scotland highlights the fragility of old empires in the 21st Century

And the beat for an independent Scotland goes on!

Secession is not unique to America!

Scotland is moving rapidly towards a referendum to leave the United Kingdom! William Wallace must be smiling …

One of my earlier articles was critical of the American news media, both the mainstream and the conservative talk shows, for their complete lack of reporting stories occurring around the world, which have real meaning for America and our future. Here's an example.

Scotland is considering secession from the United Kingdom! And, surprisingly, the English Parliament appears to have taken this course seriously! For any Scot, anywhere in the world, this is a spirit lifter! This is liberty! To be free from the occupiers, the English, at last, would be something so marvelous, something so unexpected and something so revolutionary that it could change the course of an entire world that seems to be in the midst of a one world government!

The movie *Braveheart* done by Mel Gibson, made most of America aware of the tragedy of Scotland. A people separate, a nation on the northern border of England, the Scots have been occupied for more than a thousand years. Like the American South, Scotland has always been its own nation. The Scot-Irish (Celts) were the settlers of the South, and it could be this ancestral hatred of England and its tyranny had much to do with the secession movement which swept Dixie in 1860.

Well, it seems the people of Scotland, through the election of a prime minister who ran on a pledge to offer a referendum for Scot independence, may not get a chance to voice their will. Though this referendum would be held in Scotland, the powers that be in the UK are attempting to take control of the process. Almost half of the English people oppose Scot independence.

If the process continues and there is a referendum, many pundits in England can't believe the Scots would vote to secede given the UK's government spending in Scotland. "The first question an Englishman or woman confronts on travelling through the fiscal looking glass to Scotland is: 'How on earth can they afford all this?'"

The answer to that question could be two-fold. First, all the British nuclear weapons are located in Scotland. Now, if the Scots were/are aware of the massive political battle on Long Island, New York (circa 1980-1994) around a proposed Shoreham Nuclear Plant and the billion dollar bailout required around that fiasco, they might have realized they had a trump card in British nuke politics.

The second answer as to why so much UK money is invested in Scotland has to do with energy. Scotland is the home of England's oil reserves! So, Scotland is the beneficiary of UK largesse.

Is liberty, freedom from the bloody English, worth losing their pounds? I pray, as a descendant of Scot and Irish blood that it is.

Secession in the UK, peaceful, legal departure from an occupier and oppressor — could that set a new standard of liberty for America to emulate? Could the separate states then demand the restoration of their original right as the Founders of the union, to the right of secession as articulated in the separate state resolutions, which formed the United States of America in the 1790s?

And just as importantly, how come American news no longer tells us of stories of this magnitude? On November 11, 2010, I wrote an article asking why American news, including conservative talk shows, waste their time reporting on trivia or novelty stories instead of reporting real and meaningful news? Why are we blind and deaf to what is occurring around the world?

Answer: Censorship by the ruling elite of the world, the owners of the news outlets. Control information and you control people. I have written about this also.

The potential for the world is immeasurable, also the chaos. Change is inevitable because of technology, because of the pressure of unresolved wrongs. But who will guide the change? Will it be a self-appointed elite? Will it be those who went to Harvard and Cambridge? Will it be the select few who by accident or Divine plan soar to immense wealth? Will the people have any say? Scotland is that important. Yet, is it in the news?

Scotland highlights the fragility of old empires in the 21st Century!

Scotland's quest for freedom is having affects across the globe and could ignite independence movements in the American South!

As recently as April 5, 2012, warnings from Australia indicate that Scottish independence could have much broader effects on what remains of the British empire, presently known as the United Kingdom! Australia's ties to the United Kingdom may be cut if Scotland gains her freedom!

Scotland's thirst for nationalism and independence seems quite a breath of fresh air in a world so consumed with globalism, one world government and centralization of power. And one has to wonder if the complete news blackout in America about Scotland, and the process for a referendum on liberty there is because if the Scots persist, their actions could rock the world.

A previous column I wrote back on February 7 received a fair amount of attention from readers overseas. While most seem to be pro-British and thus blast my article for bias and a lack of knowledge of the subtleties of political correctness in the UK, there are the occasional Scots who seem to illustrate the feelings of hope expressed in my article. As to my bias, I freely admit to it. The English, like the Yankees, are occupiers. They are a people not content to live within their own borders or content to shape a utopia within their own people. Instead, they see their role as savior of the world, and they did force their salvation on any people, anywhere, that they could conquer. Their military failures in America in two wars did not stop their desire to rule here. Money, huge sums of it, and the behind scenes power of a monarch are present in America today. But that's a much different, much more submerged story. Globalism is, after all, an economically driven phenomenon. The essence of it is to open global investment opportunities for large capital formations. It is quite as simple as that. And since the Queen of England sits atop one of the world's largest family fortunes, it seems only common sense to see her influence all over this newest of methods to impose British will on the world.

And if memory serves, the American Bushes are somehow blood related to English royalty; nice to keep all this money in the family and have kin so important in the ruling of *the colonies* across the pond. I wonder where Romney fits in all of this? We know he is a globalist, but I am talking about the bloodlines.

So for a descendant with Scot and Irish blood, I can't help but be fascinated by what is occurring in Scotland. Every ideology has within it the seeds of its own eventual demise. In globalism there is the optimistic view that all nations across the planet can be integrated into one global economy, a kind of Tower of Babel. That the politics, religions, history, personalities and problems associated with the more than 200 nations of the world can somehow be smoothed out, a kind of Yankee reconstruction of the whole world, so that open borders may eventually evolve into no borders.

Look at America and Mexico, where Senator Rubio (a contrived conservative of the neoconservatives) just yesterday announced his plans for immigration reform. How long will it take to remove the international boundary at the Rio Grande? Not sure, but the Bushes, Perry's, Rubio's of the US are working to make it a reality. Scotland is saying we want our boundaries and borders. We want our independence and our nationalism! In Scotland, the referendum isn't just about William Wallace, but it could be a bell rung for all who yearn to be free of their occupiers. And in the United States that could mean the South!

The globalists are enacting policies which are anti-American. Huge government debt, attempts to impose socialism, rejection of development of US energy reserves, selling off the US space industry, and a continued failure to secure the US borders are all obvious policies intended to remove the super power status of the United States. But those who manipulate US policy and are engineering the decline of a nation still in possession of vast natural resources may be once again underestimating the power of God and the eternal longing for independence. As America collapses, the example of Scotland may be that small light in the distance that brings an old dynamic back to the forefront — nationalism!

And the beat for an independent Scotland goes on!

Scotland's leaders now wrestle with how will the question be put to the Scot people in a referendum in 2014? Is America watching?

The leaders of Scotland now are deciding whether a referendum in 2014 will ask only one question: Should Scotland be independent?" Or should the people be asked two questions — one allowing Scotland to pursue more control of itself within the United Kingdom as an alternative to independence. The inclusion of the "more power" question could be seen as both an acknowledgement of the discontent within the general public of Scotland while providing a means to split the vote for freedom. England has occupied Scotland for 305 years.

A Scottish Independence Convention was formed in 2005 across political party lines. Their initial goal was to begin a public discussion about creating the circumstances to offer to the people of Scotland a referendum on Scot independence. Four political parties and sixteen council members were elected to guide the process. Important to the success of the movement was the wisdom to realize that to be successful required a agreement amongst a very broad mass of the population. The movement could not be *partisan*, but must be all of Scotland. (There is clear wisdom here for tiny groups like the Sons of Confederate Veterans who can't seem to get past thirty thousand members despite a potential market of forty million Southern descendant men.)

On April 23, 2012, the UK *Guardian* ran an exhaustive article intended to provide all the angles and aspects of the question of Scot independence. However, Severin Carrell of the *Guardian* sadly underestimates the strength of the Scot will to escape occupation of England. Unfortunately, in this article the British reporter reports that only thirty-five percent of Scots seek independence, thus establishing low expectations for the Yes Scotland Movement. But the writer does not address why the Scottish Nationalist Party (SNP) won control of the Scot Parliament in 2011, the result being the election of Alex Salmond, leader of the SNP, serving as first minister of Scotland.

On May 31 the Scottish Parliament voted in favor of Scottish independence after First Minister Salmond offered his vision of an independent nation. Scotland would retain the Queen as head of state, but would establish its own supreme court and would take a chair in the European Union. (One wonders if this is means to expand British voting power within the EU). However, Labor Party Leader Ed Miliband declares that Scots won't be British citizens if they vote for independence.

The battle for Scotland's future has myriad permutations. Australia has warned that if Scotland leaves the United Kingdom, it creates great reasons for others to consider the same.

In America, where federalism appears to be on its death bed, states may wonder if secession is a choice. If Scotland can leave England after 305 years, could some states decide to revisit the issue during the Sesquicentennial of American War Between the States? Clearly there is no single America anymore. And since the Court and Congress have all but marginalized the states, secession offers an opportunity to reassert states' rights and state sovereignty.

Section V

Modern Assets and Challenges for the South

The Internet is a New Avenue to Recreate the South ... Dixie!

Confederate History Month symbolizes continued culture war

Confederate Flag and causes of secession collide with 2012 election

The Rebel flag, a failed lesson in citizenship!

Sons of Confederate Veterans have a role in modern America

The Internet is a New Avenue to Recreate the South, Dixie!

The net could help reestablish regional identities in the virtual world; don't pass restrictive federal laws against the opportunities of the Internet.

A true patriot of the South, a man who I believe is a friend despite his disappointment in me, has repeatedly expressed his frustration and sadness at the disappearance of the Dixie which was the South; "I hate that the symbols and songs of the South are being eliminated, and replaced by things that have nothing to do with Texas, or this region of the nation."

This leader in the Sons of Confederate Veterans is just one of millions and millions of Americans who see their separate regional identities disappearing, to be replaced by some type of vanilla milquetoast, politically correct, homogenized culture which promotes meaningless diversity. Cowboys are bad, they killed Indians. Indians are bad, they are native Americans. The Catholic Church is bad because it helped the Europeans discover and civilize the rest of the world. Southerners are bad because they had slaves, sold to them by the Yankees and the Europeans. John Wayne was bad because he loved America! Ronald Reagan was bad because ... well, they haven't come up with that yet!

One of the great strengths of early America was the sovereignty, independence and character of each of the thirteen colonies. These independent countries created the United States. Each colony was different and separate from the rest. Each colony was, in effect, its own nation state when it separated from England. In fact, when King George signed the treaty ending the American Revolution, he addressed each of the thirteen colonies separately as independent nations! Few hear that in the classrooms in today's American schools, but one need only look at the treaty!

My friend's frustration and disappointment resonates with Americans all over the nation about their part of the country. Have you ever seen the movie *Fargo*? if you have, you may have been as surprised as I at their dialect, (their accent) and their lifestyles. As in the South, the weather of central northern states dictates aspects of the lives of people who live in the North.

The South is unique among all the regions of the nation. The South has its own symbol recognized around the world, the Confederate naval ensign. This flag, the Crimson Cross, represents a short-lived Confederate States of America, (1860-1865). This nation, composed of thirteen southern states (Virginia, North Carolina, South Carolina, Georgia, Florida, Mississippi, Alabama, Louisiana, Texas, Arkansas, Missouri, Tennessee and Kentucky) and two territories, the Indian Nations (Oklahoma) and Arizona (the southern halves of present-day Arizona and New Mexico), had its own Constitution, an improved variation of the United States Constitution. The South's nationality was recognized around the world, displayed on ships in ports from Shanghai to Cherbourg, France.

Presently, the United States is in its second year of the Civil War Sesquicentennial (150th) remembrance of the war. For places like Gettysburg, whose tourism nets that small town more than 300 million dollars in annual revenue and puts more than 6,000 people to work, the Sesquicentennial is an economic bonanza. Unfortunately, Southern businessmen and investors have not been as astute as the Yankees in turning history into economy prosperity. Many states in the South hide their battlefields and have done little to preserve or develop them as tourist destinations. Not even Ted Turner, who played a very minor role in a Confederate uniform in the movie *Gettysburg* gave serious consideration to investing and developing a Southern educational/tourist friendly Southern-based cultural chain of restaurants, or retail outlets throughout the South. These outlets could take advantage of the history of the defiant South, a place where all, black and white, considered themselves Southern first.

Not all of us have the resources or business acumen and ingenuity of Ted Turner. Not many of us could actually consider developing a Southern or Dixie-oriented commercial enterprise which would span the South from Virginia to Florida to Arizona. The costs would be large and there would be some risk. Only a combined, multi-media campaign created to tell the true story of the South could bring the old South back into fashion. Those running the world want nationalism dead in America. A rebirth of the South could relight the fires of Americanism, and well, that's not in vogue in London or Beijing.

That brings us to the Internet. With very little expense, imaginative, creative, well-read individuals can construct a Southern infrastructure. On the Internet, the history of the old South can be brought to life and, just as importantly, the concepts of liberty, self-reliance, a pioneer spirit, Christianity and Southern nationalism in the modern sense can be explored and discussed.

Technologies developed during the Cold War (1945-1991), which have been transformed into commercial goliaths in the early twenty-first century, offer a new opportunity to reinstate Southern values and traditions in the modern world. It is on the Internet that the New Confederacy can emerge.

This is not a direct answer to my friend's disappointment. But it does provide a means for like-minded people to congregate and work on building an electronic colony complete with Southern culture, and integrated into what remains of the old South. And who knows, should the activity on the Internet indicate that tens of millions of Americans (some 50 to 80 million are descendants of Confederate gray) want to embrace the values of the old South, now that slavery is dead and racism a despised social fault of all regions of America, maybe a future Ted Turner will see the investment opportunities of creating a new Southern styled, Disney-like complex complete with a Christian value set and an invigorated Dixie spirit.

But in the Culture War, which exists every day in America, people opposed to the South are behind the first step in legislation to kill free speech on the internet. The STOP ONLINE PIRACY ACT could kill this new avenue to reclaim the original American diversity of the regions of the nation. Don't let Congress rob the opportunities for freedom of speech and cultural diversity by imposing their will on the Internet! Call your Congressman and tell him to vote no on this act. And after you do, settle down for some supper.

Hey, pass the black-eyed peas, will ya? How 'bout some of that chicken-fried steak? And oh, I must have some of those corn fritters! Can we still get the Grand Ole Opry?

Confederate History Month symbolizes continued culture war

Governor McConnell's proclamation stirs re-engagement of social civil war in America.

Can the government of the United States go too far? Is there any way, besides taxation's effect on the economy, to know if and when the federal government of the United States has gone too far in stripping away the individual liberty of its citizens?

The rhetorical volleys which have echoed across America about Governor McConnell's proclamation in support of Confederate History Month clearly demonstrate the wide differences between Americans on the very broadest range of issues. The republic of Republics, created by our Founding Fathers, is no longer alive. The American Civil War did much more than preserve the Union and end slavery. It started the process by which the Herculean efforts of so many early American patriots to create a land of liberty were erased. Not just the independence of the thirteen independent colonies, but the independence and liberty of the individual citizen.

Alexis d'Tocqueville's observations about the struggle between liberty and equality were both accurate and prophetic. Material equality has risen to paramount importance and through taxation, regulation, and the destruction of state sovereignty is virtually obliterating the liberties articulated in the Bill of Rights.

This is not the America Washington, Lee, Jefferson, Patrick Henry, Madison and Mason intended. The Tenth Amendment, the guide to how America was to deal with questions yet asked, has been set aside. The federal government, through the US Supreme Court has decided what powers it will seize and which ones it will leave to the states. These latter powers are few and temporary because in the progressive view of the *living* Constitution, the Court can at any time revisit a question and arbitrarily change the foundational law of the land, seizing power and expanding the role of government. Even the very foundations of our nation, "life, liberty and the pursuit of happiness" are not immune as is demonstrated by the Court's decision to forfeit the right to life to the innocent unborn in Roe vs. Wade.

Abortion is the modern-day equivalent to the slavery of the past. It is another blemish on the character of the American nation.

America is not the nation we hoped it would be. And it is as much "mom and pop's" fault as it is the fault of the powerful. Americans have been unable to live up to the responsibility of citizenship. Americans have not guarded their citizenship, but have allowed any transient the right to influence American policy through the vote, as a lobbyist, as a special interest. We have not cherished the gift given to us by our Creator.

The grand experiment is in serious mortal danger. Our nation has drifted from the Bible, from its originating faith in Christ. Our nation allows our public airwaves to be used by Satan to spread immorality. Our opposition to the creation of a national church has been turned into separation of God from the American people.

When defining right from wrong, there is no other source more appropriate for the United States of America then the Christian Bible. Yet, when ethics in the American classroom is discussed, of the many sources quoted, the Bible is not one of them. Right and wrong is created from human experience and *knowledge*, not divine inspiration.

And if the discussion of right and wrong in the classroom is absent the Bible, then can we be surprised that freedom of speech includes pornography? Can we be surprised public prayer at high school football games is a crime!

The Culture War in America rages. It is not over. Sarah Palin is our hope. She rises from the masses. She is us. She is not manipulated by the wisdom of the Ivy League. She is the quintessential American and she scares the heck out of the progressives whose arguments will collapse when placed under the light of reality. Her anchor is in American history and in living life on the frontier. Her successful efforts on behalf of the Alaskan people in negotiations with the oil companies are testimony not only to her intelligence but to her political acumen.

The fight rages on. We can be a better nation and better people. We can reclaim our inheritance as Americans.

Thank you, Governor McConnell, for recognizing the patriots of old Virginia. Thank you for having the courage to say that, though imperfect, the Confederates of Virginia and the South are worth remembering. No doubt, from their heavenly perch, they watch with interest the results of Lincoln's victory.

The Confederate Flag and causes of secession collide with 2012 election

Rick Perry and Texas bring history to today's election in some very important and major ways.

If the issue of the approval for the Sons of Confederate Veterans specialty license plates revolved only around the honorable service of the men who served the Confederacy defending Texas from Union attack, the debate would be brief, the plates already approved.

In the modern world, the battle flag of the Army of Northern Virginia is the single most recognized symbol of a region of the United States (the South) in the whole world. The crimson field framing the St. Andrews Cross has flown over Berlin when the Iron Curtain dividing Germany fell. And it flew in Afghanistan when the Soviet Union was driven from its occupation of that nation.

The Confederate Battle Flag is an international symbol of defiance, individual liberty and regional unity. While some white supremacist groups have attempted to abscond with the colors, the history and lineage of the colors place it on a platform of honor and sacrifice which cannot pervert its original meaning.

Though American revisionist historians in the late twentieth century attempted to corrupt the reputations of the men who fought under the crimson flag, Generals Robert E. Lee, Thomas "Stonewall" Jackson, Patrick Cleburne and many other Southern patriots remain a noble corps of Christian Americans seeking an alternative government for Dixie. And it is this spirit and pride which drives the 2,400 members of the Texas Division of the Sons of Confederate Veterans to seek approval for the specialty license plate.

But, alas, those who oppose approval of the plates have attacked the meaning of the Confederate Battle Flag on grounds not directly associated with its original purpose. Therefore, in order to defend the values of the men who fought under the Confederate Battle Flag, the following article has been penned here on Rebel Mountain in East Texas.

God, Himself, may be the organizing dynamic behind the controversy in Texas. This article attempts to connect the history of secession and an alternative American Constitution with the present-day troubles and frustrations of our nation. The issues the United States faces today, and the normally ignored causes of secession in 1860, combined with the creation of the Confederate States of America, (CSA) provide a startling illustration of the relevance of the Southern nation to today's troubles. The CSA offered an alternative America, one which has much relevance today and could provide a route to a new American future.

The Sons of Confederate Veterans (SCV), the Texas Division, the Confederate States of America and the South are all benefitting from the media interest associated in the division application for Texas specialty license plates. Governor Rick Perry's decision to enter and compete in the Republican primary contest for the nomination for president of the United States has brought the American Civil War Sesquicentennial and our division's efforts to secure a license plate to the fore of the current national campaign. We see repeatedly news agencies within Texas and across the nation are contacting local and brigade SCV representatives, and to some extent, we are participating in interviews about the issue.

I have not seen any of the interviews, and since I have not seen a standardized fact sheet produced and distributed across the division, or at the national level, I can only assume the interviews are in no way coordinated or developed to send the same message. Instead, local men, with varying degrees of historical and political knowledge, are doing the best they can to respond.

During this ongoing series of events, we see our political opponents are able to hold press conferences, attract media attention, and organize their anti-Southern messages for the general public.

And of course, the Perry Campaign is doing what it feels necessary to react. Again, since I have seen no national reporting of the event nor have I seen Governor Perry make any comments, I can only presume the Perry campaign is doing the best it can to avoid the issue. Governor Perry and his operatives are running for president and do not feel a need to open up a can of worms by re-teaching American history and governance. Therefore, we cannot anticipate their reaction on this issue to be supportive of recreating an American foundation.

Further, Governor Perry's avoidance of a detailed discussion of the causes of secession indicates just how non-conservative Governor Rick Perry is. You see, an open discussion of the application for the license plates provides a very unique, very American approach to the current campaign issues which face our nation, everything from open borders with Mexico, to industry bailouts, national health care and the role of states. The topic of the license plate does provide an opportunity for a discussion of the modern role of the Tenth Amendment, but that is not something any of the Republican candidates have embraced as a centerpiece of their campaign.

Our opponents are attacking the Sons of Confederate Veterans' application for specialty plates for one and only one reason — racism. They connect the Confederate Battle Flag to the slavery of 1861-1865 and to the racism of the mid-20th century. They tie the Confederate Battle Flag to the KKK and other white supremacist groups and, by doing so, attempt to strip away support from conservative America. This is their stratagem and it is neither unanticipated nor ineffective. Many minorities, who have no real economic or social plans which they can openly explain and discuss, use racism as their lone card to play.

For our opponents, this is a *bread and butter* no work issue. For decades they have used standardized assaults on the South to build and maintain name recognition for themselves and unify their cohorts with mindless proclamations which occupy air time.

But for us, the 50-80 million Americans whose ancestors fought for the South, for those people who proudly belong to the Sons of the Confederate Veterans and want to see the state of Texas issue our specialty license plates, we have an arsenal of important political, historical and social lines of argument which should be presented to the American people.

For years, decades, we have argued the South left the Union for a number of reasons. However, we have done a relatively poor job of painting the full picture, of illustrating exactly what the differences were between North and South. Today, now, in this time, when the United States of America is seeing its national identity destroyed by both the Democratic and Republican parties and global special interests, this argument concerning the Texas license plates is brought before the people of America by God. He, the Almighty God, has brought forward the history of one hundred and fifty years, and the causes of secession, and the alternative American democracy of the Confederate States of America so that Americans at the beginning of the twenty-first century can see that America could avoid much of what is occurring today. The problems we face are not inherent in our nation. No, instead, because of the War and the decisions made by Congress and the Supreme Court after 1865, we have chosen the malaise and complications we face today.

As the Lt. Commander of the Texas Division, Sons of Confederate Veterans (responsible for Heritage Defense), I have given much thought to the points of argument I will now present for consideration by the members of the Sons of Confederate Veterans, by Texans, and by today's Americans. I offer these thoughts not as a line of argument to secure passage of the Texas license plates, but as a broader line of logic for the future of America herself.

For generations, the issue of slavery has been an intellectual black hole, which has acted as an impenetrable cloud covering secession and an alternative American democracy. Slavery was used to distract students from considering an alternative American government. There have been no serious discussions of an alternative United States because all of the Confederate modifications to the US Constitution have been overshadowed by one issue — slavery. Slavery has been used to prevent students and Americans from considering all of the alternatives included in the Confederate Constitution. The evil of slavery has stood alone as the soul difference between the shattered Union and the rebel South.

But the differences which were incorporated into the new Confederate Constitution were anticipatory of many of the largest problems we face today. The changes to the Confederate Constitution reflected a region and people who knew the formation of the United States some seventy years earlier, and who wanted to preserve those foundations. Had we done so, America's future today would be much different.

So to begin this discussion of an alternative American democracy and the Southern nation, let's quickly, completely, and without reservation condemn the institution of slavery for what it was: an American sin against man which should have never been brought to these shores by the Europeans and Americans from the northeast who operated the ships and markets that transported and sold slaves within the United States.

Slavery was *NOT* a uniquely Southern thing in the 16th century. The slaves brought to the western world were brought by the European powers and deposited all along the coasts of North and South America and the islands of the Caribbean. The United Kingdom, the Netherlands, Spain, France (which continue to try to rule the world to this day), facilitated the slave trade. It was the *globalism* of their time, an economic system intended to reap the benefits of the new world. Yes, the South did participate, and yes, the sin is as much that of the people of the South as the people of the North or the people of South America. But slavery was not a uniquely Southern thing. Like abortion today, where fifty million American souls have perished, slavery was an American thing.

Unlike the Northerners, Southerners hoped to build an agricultural, rural nation. Slavery was seen as the foundational means to help build this reality. Northerners, who early realized slavery could not work above the Mason-Dixon line, did not free their slaves, or return them to Africa. Instead, they sold them south for profit. Slavery would eventually end in the North, after the Revolutionary War, but it was not due to northern Christianity and mercy, but as a result of economic necessity.

So let us here accept that slavery was a national sin, one equally caused by North and South, condemn it and move to a discussion of the political and legal alternatives offered by the Confederate States of America in their Constitution.

With slavery condemned, let us now look at the alternative America of the Confederate Constitution. It is important to recall that the founders of the American Constitution saw the central government as a necessary evil. A central element behind the creation of the Constitution was this fear of an uncontrolled central government.

When considering where power came from, the Southern perspective first finds political sovereignty in God. From God, sovereignty passes to each individual. The individual surrenders a degree of sovereignty to the state. And then finally, the states shed a small piece of their power to the central government. To further insure that the federal government could NOT exercise power in certain areas, the Bill of Rights was offered simultaneously to the Constitution for approval by the states.

For a more in-depth knowledge of the early United States, the fear of a powerful central government and the roots of Southern political thinking, I recommend to you *The South Was Right!* by James and Walter Kennedy.

The Confederate Constitution would incorporate a series of changes, which when taken together created a new government with different character. The major changes within the Constitution include:

1. The inclusion of God in the Preamble where the Southern nation called for the protection and guidance of Almighty God. This open inclusion of a Christian God in the Preamble could very likely influence the moral aspects of national law throughout the centuries and avoid what is presently known as the doctrine of "separation of church and state."

2. The hope that a "less than perfect union" could survive by not challenging the power of the states.

3. That secession was an inherent right of the state and, therefore, the ultimate check on central power.

4. That citizenship came only through birth within the Confederacy.

5. That the single six-year term president was given sufficient power to operate the government and most importantly control spending.

6. That Congress was prohibited from using earmarks to pass legislation.

7. That two-thirds of Congress must approve spending above that proposed by the president.

8. That the central government was prohibited from providing bailouts for industry and was prohibited from acting on behalf of individual businesses,

9. That the Confederacy was much more attuned to the global economy and sought trade as the source of many consumer goods.

A full discussion of these and other changes within the Constitution by learned professors at schools of higher learning could provide modern-day America a whole new direction for national development.

What the Southern point of view offered was liberty, state integrity, local control, a fully integrated Christian faith into citizenship and, most importantly, the preservation of values of George Washington, Thomas Jefferson and the other Southern founders of our nation.

In the coming years the Sons of Confederate Veterans will be faced with a choice. As a not-for-profit organization we are responsible for the *Charge* given to us by Lt. General Stephan D. Lee. In that *Charge* we are asked to vindicate the *Cause*. In the past vindication has meant ceremonies at cemeteries, marching in parades, participating in living histories, and other relatively benign historical events. It is my view that to live up to the *Charge*, members of the Sons of Confederate Veterans must become politically active in reclaiming the ground which was originally America.

There is much to do, but men of Southern heritage are men who can do much when working with God as their partner. So let's get these plates approved and take one more step down the road of the Sesquicentennial.

The Rebel flag, a failed lesson in citizenship!

In Texas, a small group of patriots lost the fight for a license plate without firing a shot!

Thirteen states (Virginia, North Carolina, South Carolina, Georgia, Florida, Alabama, Mississippi, Tennessee, Louisiana, Arkansas, Texas, Kentucky and Missouri) and two territories (the Indian territory which was Oklahoma and Arizona) composed the Confederate States of America. Nine of those states have specialty license plates honoring the Sons of Confederate Veterans (SCV). In some of these states, it was the courts who decided in favor of freedom of speech and equal treatment under the law for the granting of the license plates.

But this week the Texas Department of Transportation decided to refuse the license plate to the Texas Division of the SCV. The timing of this issue was combined with the Civil War 150th Sesquicentennial Remembrance, the presidential aspirations of Texas Governor Rick Perry, and a United States as divided over issues as it was back in 1860!

This is not the first defeat for the SCV in Texas. When George Bush was governor, in the dark of the night he sent government agents to remove plaques honoring the United Daughters of the Confederacy and the South from Texas government buildings! The SCV took Texas to court in a lawsuit, and after years of deliberation and what could be about $200,000 in legal fees, the court decided Governor Bush operated outside the law, but refused to order the plaques returned to their locations. The SCV lost.

Also in Texas, the same Texas Department of Transportation has blocked SCV efforts to use a billboard on the public roads!

Florida has also been the site of a recent SCV court defeat … this one concerning their application for specialty license plates in that state.

When you are a politically incorrect group, you don't get the fairness politically correct groups like ethnic minorities or homosexuals get. You just kind of get urinated on by the courts, who tell you it's raining. Though to be fair, ethnic minority groups and gays have learned and have used all the tools of civil disobedience and political participation.

For the members of the Sons of Confederate Veterans in Texas, their effort to secure the plates was conducted as *inside baseball* by their state leadership. A strategy decision was made *NOT* to engage in the normal political rules of engagement. A group normally attempts to influence government policy. However, the SCV did not do a letter-writing campaign to their state's elected representatives or a phone bank to those same representatives. The *rebels* did not hold rallies or parades to garner public support for their effort to secure the license plates. The Texas Division did not hold press conferences or go on the offense to offer their spokesmen for prime television or radio interviews. The Texas Division did not raise or allocate money for an advertising campaign. No effort was made to discuss the issue with the governor, or approach colleges and universities to hold discussions or debates between SCV spokesmen and college professors or students. None of the normal efforts to petition government were attempted. The Texas SCV commander had decided the course and no amount of internal debate within the division would change his mind. He had settled on silence and silence from the 2,500 men of the Texas Division was to be the course.

The commander was so sure the efforts before the Texas Transportation Committee would fail that in June he got the approval of the Division Board of Directors to go ahead with a lawsuit when Texas turned down their application.

A recent estimate indicates that somewhere between 50 and 80 million Americans are descendants of Confederate gray. Yet, only thirty thousand men belong to the Sons of Confederate Veterans! Why is that?

The Sons of Confederate Veterans is a fraternal ancestral organization charged with vindicating the *Cause* for which almost one million Southern men fought. Each year at their national reunion, the SCV condemns white supremacist groups. Many within the SCV condemn slavery and tell of the battles within the South, exclusive of Yankee interference, to end the institution before 1860. In addition, many in the SCV are interested in the black support for the Southern nation, which came in the form of serving in the military, and maintaining the Southern economy during the war. Three and a half million slaves were more than a third of the almost nine million Southerners who left the Union. No slave revolts occurred during the war. No actions which could have paralyzed the South occurred.

The Sons of Confederate Veterans argue the war was not about slavery, but about the preservation of the original Constitution. Few Americans realize the Lincoln Administration followed very shortly after the creation of the Republican Party. Northerners were looking for a stronger federal government and they used the war as a means to that end. Following the War the XIV Amendment to the Constitution would be rammed down the throat of the Southern states. To reenter the Union, the Southern states were required to pass this amendment which expanded and centralized federal power. Expansion of the federal government which led to a federal department of education, Obama health care, the income tax, social security and the overwhelming assortment of federal rules and regulations all began at Appomattox.

The Confederate Constitution of 1861, modified to better reflect the original Constitution, made several major changes including:

a. Calling on the protection and guidance of Almighty God (Christian) in the Preamble.
b. Term limiting the president to one six-year term.
c. Reasserting the sovereignty of the states.
d. Severely limiting the power of Congress to spend money *vis-a-vis* the president.
e. Prohibiting industry bailouts and congressional earmarks.
f. Toughening rules of citizenship, voting, and holding office.

In many respects the Sons of Confederate Veterans are the forerunners of today's Tea Party! The membership of the SCV embraces a deep belief in the original Constitution and the concept of "consent of the governed." But, unfortunately, unlike other not-for-profit organizations like the NRA, the veterans' organizations, minority groups, Kiwanis, Rotary, Chamber of Commerce, AARP, AMAC, etc., the SCV membership has not been organized and trained to participate in the American political system.

When one considers that 50 to 80 million Americans are descendants of Confederate soldiers and sailors, one would think organizing politically would be an excellent means for growing the organization. Today's America suffers from many of the problems identified by Southern statesmen back in the mid-19th century. The Sons of Confederate Veterans with approximately 1,000 local organizations across the nation routinely hold presentations discussing aspects of American history ignored in America's classrooms.

Local SCV organizations are called camps, and they do a tremendous amount of civic work each year. The men from these camps participate in living history demonstrations, and reenactments. They participate in local parades across the South and are invited into public schools during the school year to tell the children about the Confederate soldier and the stories of the South, which are seldom told in school books. The local camps routinely host authors and storytellers at their monthly meetings. So the men of the SCV are already pretty busy.

But in Texas they may have learned that the responsibilities of citizenship require they must learn the business of governing and how to participate in order to influence the decisions of their government. Citizenship is work, lots of it. When one realizes that only about 60 percent of Americans are registered to vote and only half of the registered voters vote, it demonstrates that many, if not most, Americans, don't participate in citizenship at all. This might explain why 98 percent of incumbents are reelected and why America is rapidly headed towards $17,000,000,000,000 in debt!

The Sons of Confederate Veterans have a role in modern America

America faces a crossroads very similar to those prior to Fort Sumter. More government, less nationalism, maybe socialism, which way do we go?

What is this guy talking about?

Well, I will try to explain. It will only take ten short paragraphs.

The Sons of Confederate Veterans (SCV) is a fraternal organization composed of male descendants of the men who served in the Confederate Armed Forces during the War for Southern Independence. Their emblems include the controversial Confederate Battle Flag. Their core responsibility is articulated in a *Charge* given to them by Lt. General Stephen D. Lee, which calls on them to defend the heritage, honor and reputation of the Confederate soldier and the cause for which they fought.

The cause they fought for was individual liberty, states' rights, the original Constitution and the right to secede. In essence, Confederates fought an aggressive Union which would not allow the states to exercise an accepted right of secession. This right had been exercised by all the original states when they withdrew from the government of the Articles of Confederation and entered the present-day United States of America. Further, the Tenth Amendment reserved all powers not addressed in the Constitution to the states and people respectively. And lastly, the new union was formed as each individual state entered the Union.

So, despite the military victory of Grant and Sherman, and despite the victor's interpretation towards secession, the fact is that secession remains a right of the states and a political alternative, which some day will most likely be exercised.

Why the SCV deserves a chair, not at the table but right next to it, is so today's policymakers see the colors of secession — the Confederate Battle Flag — as they attempt to find the future for America.

America is caught in a vortex of highly controversial issues, many with no real compromise. You either kill an unborn infant or you allow it to be born. For the infant, there is no middle ground. You either allow homosexual marriage ... even if you call it something else or you don't. Either a person has a right to health care or they don't.

In the past, liberals have sold policy initiatives in half loaves, calling for compromise. But today, that sales strategy is burned out. We have seen the compromises develop into full blown, expensive, ineffective policies. We have seen compromise go the way of the Missouri Compromise as socialism now raises its ugly head in the form of national health care and government ownership of private business.

Americans are done with hearing about how government can solve the problems, when all government does is continually make new problems, add taxes, and never accomplishes much. Further, Americans have watched the federal government act negligently with respect to its primary duty, i.e., protect the homeland at the border. The tens of millions of illegal immigrants have only expanded the need for government social services, increased health care costs and challenges, overwhelmed our education infrastructure and filled our prisons. Illegal drugs flow over the border like a rushing river.

Whether you are a Democrat watching blue states vote red or Republicans waiting their turn to take over the reins of government, one thing is clear. Americans are out of patience and want the solutions they have repeatedly demanded. America is a new America, not the America of the mid-20th century or the world leader of the Cold War. We are now just one nation among many.

Are we a great nation? We can be. Should we lead in the world? Sometimes. But we are not the superpower of an earlier era. We are no longer the wealthiest nation. We no longer have excess money to fix every problem in the world. We have to make choices. Real choices with real ramifications. Washington is not where those answers are. They had their chance, and through Clinton-Bush-Obama, they have demonstrated they can't do it, are headed in the wrong direction, and we don't want 'em any more.

The SCV should be present so as to remind politicians the American people don't have endless patience. The SCV is the very best living example, as the War for Southern Independence Sesquicentennial rapidly approaches, that if the federal government can't find a way, the states and the people will.

Section VI

The Sesquicentennial 2010 - 2015

In the Sesquicentennial, the story of the South should be boldly told

Who owns January 19?

Let's create a Confederate holiday

The Trans-Mississippi Theater … the unknown Civil War

History seeks a benefactor

In the Sesquicentennial, the story of the South should be boldly told

Many forms of censorship are being used to silence the story of the South and to promote politically correct Yankee history!

The years 2010 through 2015 mark the 150th Anniversary and remembrance of a war within the United States which changed forever the meaning of the US Constitution and the aspirations of the Founding Fathers. The war most commonly referred to as the Civil War could just as easily be called the War of the Constitution.

For my lifetime, the past half century and a little, revisionists, as the most ardent of Yankee victors, have been attempting to steal away into the dark caverns of library and museum archives and into private collections, the real causes of secession and war. Recently, I am told an article in *USA Today* reported many museums of the War are rewriting their exhibits to make them more politically correct. I am told the story said this was being done because of poor visitation and a need to increase revenues through increased attendance and possibly federalized government funding! So the story of the South, the story of liberty and freedom is being concealed so that more space can be given to slavery and the abuse of the African-American. For me, there is and should be room for both.

The Culture War ongoing within the United States is not about promoting the history of a people who were abused. It is about using the sin of the United States — slavery to hide the fact the South did not secede because of slavery which was protected in the Constitution. The South's secession was because the people of that time saw in the election of a president the end to the confederation originally constructed under the Constitution and the beginnings of what we would become today's disaster, called America. They foresaw massive federal spending and taxation. They saw the sovereign states becoming nothing more than administrative districts. They saw Washington's warning about international involvement being cast aside. And they saw the power of bluebloods, presently represented by former Governor Mitt Romney, as desirous of replacing liberty and Christianity with materialism and consumerism.

In the article, which I saw only parts of, one museum spokesman said museums had to change, to become more in step with modern perceptions if they were to attract visitors. Here again, we see censorship in a form not recognizable, mostly because the general public would not even know it was occurring. But, for example at Gettysburg, the new federal Visitor's Center focuses on the intellectual black hole of slavery, not telling of the real and true differences between the US and Confederate constitutions.

By the way, Gettysburg's economic development reports tell us this small Pennsylvania town earns more than 300 million dollars per year in tourist revenues, which employ more than 6,000 people. In the South, battlefields are hidden. Southern states' tourism efforts at their visitor centers on the Interstates do as much as possible to hide information about Southern battlefields. Southern pride turned to Southern shame. Again, where are the heritage defense groups? Off doing whatever they do, but certainly not pressuring elected officials to promote Southern history!

Southern heritage groups, like the Sons of Confederate Veterans, help perpetuate the black hole which forcefully pulls all inquiries about the reasons for secession to slavery because they refuse to stand up and condemn slavery as the sin it was and is. The causes for secession are best articulated in the differences between the Confederate Constitution and the US. Much of what Rush Limbaugh, Sean Hannity and other conservative talk show hosts say today could be policy initiatives from the CSA! But few even realize there was a Confederate Constitution which offered a different, alternative view of America, which would have avoided many of today's most troublesome problems.

It is impossible to introduce the Confederate Constitution to the uninformed unless you first condemn slavery as a sin. Once slavery is condemned as wrong, once the absolute tragedy of African-Americans is recognized and addressed, then proponents of the Southern point of view of an alternative America could be explored and much good taken from it. And for those who now condemn the South and the Confederacy for slavery, they would then have to talk about God at the governing table, stricter financial controls, tight controls on citizenship, nationalism, regionalism, states' rights and the benefits of diversity as reflected in the actual wants and needs of people in each state.

The North, the bluebloods of New England, are not free of their participation in the sin of slavery. It was the European powers and the Northern merchantmen who participated in the slave trade. It was the Yankees who initially financed and brought the slaves to America. They were sold from Maine to Georgia — the original profits of the slave trade going almost exclusively to New York and Boston! The thousands and thousands of Africans who died on slave ships, died in the hands of the Europeans and Yankees, not the South.

Slavery ended in the North when it did not work, but prospered in the South where warmer climates and agricultural pursuits demand inexpensive labor. Later Northern and European textile factories would employ tens of thousands, maybe hundreds of thousands, in the process of transforming slave grown-and-picked cotton into the fabrics which would make shirts, pants, coats and dresses.

Southern museums are moving away from Southern history, not because it is not profitable in an open market, but because government funds and the fashion of historiography today condemn the South. Again, the Southern heritage organizations are nowhere to be seen. Passive and impotent, they do not do their duty and work to influence government policy in education and the parks. Censorship raises its ugly head and darkness pervades the halls of learning and groups like the SCV, charged with vindicating the *Cause*, file lawsuits over license plates but refuse to organize letter campaigns or visitations to elected representatives with a list of demands like many other not-for-profit groups do. The Culture War is being won by the left, because the right is living in the past, instead of the present.

What we don't know can't hurt us is the belief of the liberal or the progressive. If you were to learn for the first time that secession was a right acknowledged by both Northern and Southern states at the time of the adoption of the present-day Constitution, then you might ask questions like why? And you might learn that secession as a right is the most effective tool against an activist court. Had secession been an acknowledged right in the 1970s, Roe vs. Wade could never have been decided as it was — the Bible Belt would have left along with much of the more conservative West.

The Sesquicentennial provides a real opportunity for Americans to reevaluate the course we took. Is this where we want to be? Is this where the Founder's intended us? If you would like more information about the real differences between North and South, the real causes for secession, try the Abbeville Institute in South Carolina. And when you visit museums, flood the curators and employees with questions about President Jefferson Davis, the Confederate Constitution, and the political differences between the two regions apart from slavery. The looks you will get will be priceless as these highly degreed bureaucrats stumble to answer questions they never expected.

A great business opportunity rests in telling the story of the underdog, the Rocky of the War for Southern Independence. Use modern technologies, modern hands on interactive methods, but tell the story of a people being oppressed by the federal government, overtaxed, and responsible for financing projects which benefitted them not. Yes, absolutely include the story of the African-Americans, but tell the real story. Tell of the horrors of slavery, but tell of the great bonds between Southerners, white and black. Tell of who operated the entire Southern home front while the whites were off defending home and hearth. Tell of the rape of African-Americans by Yankee invaders. Turn the lights on! Tell all of American history — not just those aspects financed by the bluebloods of New England.

The South has a wonderful, full, tragic story. Tell it all. It's good business.

Who owns January 19th?

Two great Americans were born on January 19th, was there a purpose to God's plan?

April is Confederate History Month in the South, and each year when this comes round, the news media (looking for ratings) invents another story in order to generate an audience. This year it is occurring in Palestine, Texas, where a band of men in the local camp of the Sons of Confederate Veterans approached their county elected officials and asked to fly the First Confederate Flag at the courthouse. Their request was approved and the controversy started only moments after the flag-raising ceremony.

Texas was the seventh state to secede. And Texas, unlike other states, actually had a referendum where the qualified voters of the state went to the ballot box to vote on the question of secession. In Texas, more than seventy percent voted to leave the Union. A series of ten major fires in cities and towns all across the state, reportedly caused by abolitionists connected with John Brown, had something to do with the vote.

Six more states, (North Carolina, Virginia, Tennessee, Arkansas, Kentucky and Missouri) and two territories (Oklahoma and Arizona) would leave the Union and join the Confederacy after President Lincoln called for seventy-five thousand volunteers to invade the South. The war would rage for four years. More than 623,000 Americans would die in the contest. Brother would fight brother; father against son.

Blacks would fight for both sides, though that isn't mentioned much.

Slavery was certainly an issue, as was terrorism, states' rights, or rather, the sovereignty of the state over the federal government. Secession had long been recognized as a right of the state. Secession was taught as a right of the states at West Point, the leading college in the nation at the time. The tenth amendment, in giving all unstated powers to the states and the people respectively, was the legal basis for secession.

So a war happened and the South lost. America was reunited.

But is it reunited?

From 1865 to about 1960, the politically correct telling of the war in the South revolved around the heroes of the war, Robert E. Lee, Stonewall Jackson, et. al. Confederate Heroes Day was a state holiday. In many states, January 19th, Lee's birthday, was the holiday.

Then, with the civil rights movement, the black voice rose in the chorus which is America. And after a time, a holiday was set to recognize one great American, a black American, Dr. Martin Luther King, Jr., his birthday, January 15th is observed on the third Monday in January. And so General Lee is pushed aside for King when the two dates fall together.

And that seems to be the way it is in America today. It's either King or Lee. But America says it's for diversity. America says it's for the right of all.

If that's true, shouldn't January 19 be a King-Lee holiday?

Both men were great Americans. Both men lived by a Christian God's words. Both men sacrificed much for their people. Both men were national leaders in their own times.

One thing is for sure. Neither man is going away, nor are their descendants. And, in my view, neither should.

America is in tough times. The federal system of government as created by the winners of the Civil War is crumbling. Socialism seems to be creeping in, and there seems to be no real alternative. And yet, there once was an alternative American government, a much more fiscally conservative central government where domestic issues were in the hands of the states. People could choose how they wanted to live by where they chose to live.

America is now three hundred million. Many issues like abortion offer no compromise. Fifty million infant Americans have been slaughtered as a result of an activist court decision. Most of those who died through abortion were black.

I would submit that if America is not big enough to appreciate both Lee and King, it will not survive. Lee and King provide a poignant example of the difference in America, but certainly not the only one.

America has the potential to be the city on the hill, but if it be God's will that we be that city, leaders from all communities will have to work towards a Lee-King holiday!

Let's create a Confederate holiday!

Economics drives politics; if consumers buy Southern, the South will rise!

Let's create a Confederate holiday!

One of the great lessons of America is how people spend their money shapes our society! Where money goes, politically correct follows.

Please consider what I have written above. Take a moment. Think about it. Do you agree that if people spend money on something it becomes accepted in America? If you said yes, than please consider what I propose below!

Economics and money drive what goes on in our world. In many respects economics drives politics. There are between 50-80 million Americans with Southern blood who go back to the days of the Confederate States of America! That is a huge potential market. Southern music, food, art, history, toys, are popular items. Even with Yankees! Three million people a year visit Gettysburg, generating 300 million dollars a year in tourism for that little town. In this new virtual world of the Internet, regions of the nation don't have to become homogenized into some vanilla America. We can survive. But we have to think in terms of economics. What makes money stays around.

April is Confederate History Month in the South. So I propose that like other holidays in America, you consider purchasing a gift for someone during Confederate History Month and maybe even a card. But I propose both the gift and the card be oriented towards our Southern history and heritage. Now this will start small, because I know many who read this just won't have the vision to see. But Christmas started small, Valentine's Day, etc. They all started small and now are major marketing periods each year.

Want to see Confederate Flags sold in Walmart? Then buy one! Want to see Confederate cards in Hallmark? Create a demand for them. Go to Hallmark and ask if they have any! Want to hear Southern heritage music on the radio? Buy a Jed Marum CD and send it to your favorite radio station!

Now, I won't mislead. I do have a Commissary at the Confederate War College where you can buy Confederate items. And sure, I would love for you to stop by the Commissary and place an order! But there are other places to make purchases: Dixie Outfitters would be a great place! But don't just purchase something. Purchase a gift, wrap it in Confederate wrapping paper and give it to a child or someone you really care about!

Let's talk to our kids. Let's ask the creative ones to consider developing Confederate wrapping paper and Confederate holiday cards! Let's begin to listen to men like Jed Marum, The Majors, and others who create Southern music. Let's buy books produced by pro-Southern creators like Charles Hayes who authored a comic strip book about the war with a Southern perspective!

Some of these products are available at The Confederate War College Commissary. So sure I would love for you to stop by and make a purchase of a gift. But spread the word. Let's start something which continues and grows. Let's start something which attracts the attention of people with money to invest. The South owns the majority of the battlefields, the majority of places connected to the Great War. These could be economic engines for the region! We need a Confederate Disneyland! Remember Six Flags had a Southern area when it first opened! If you go to Six Flags, ask for that area! When they appear confused, point them back to their own history as an amusement park!

Prove there is a market for Southern goods. Spend your money on your heart. Buy Southern.

The Trans-Mississippi Theater, the unknown Civil War

In a vast area west of the Mississippi River, the war took on a different form with a different cast of characters.

The American Civil War or War for Southern Independence is experiencing its Sesquicentennial (150th) Remembrance between the years 2010-2015. This era of American history may be the most read about and the most interesting to Americans of all generations. The struggle between the advocates of the original Constitution and those seeking to reshape the role of the federal government is the beginning point for the America of today. Thousands of books have been written about the causes of secession, Lincoln's commitment to preserve the Union, the actual war years and reconstruction. Millions of Americans annually visit the hundreds of battlefields and historic locations connected to the war.

But despite all of this activity and interest, there are areas of study within the War which receive relatively minor attention, whose stories rest undisturbed beneath layers of dust. Two of these areas are the Confederate Navy and the Trans-Mississippi Theater. The size, scope and success of the Confederate Navy is a story equal in excitement and daring to General Robert E. Lee and the Army of Northern Virginia. Confederate naval commanders equaled Stuart, Forrest, Morgan and Mosby in personal bravery, tactical brilliance and commitment. The CSN sheds a light on the Confederacy, which opens the struggle to a global scale while highlighting the ingenuity and strategic genius of the South's maritime leadership. It is an area you should consider visiting if you are a student of the era. It will change your appreciation of the South!

However, another area seldom studied and poorly understood is the Trans-Mississippi Theater. This is the vast area west of the Mississippi River which runs to the Pacific Ocean. It is a completely different war with untold stories of heroism and sacrifice. It is a war reliant on horses for mobility, where distance and geography are very different from the Eastern and Western (central) theaters.

The Trans-Mississippi Theater adds aspects to the war seldom considered east of the Mississippi. Through this brief essay I would like to introduce you to some of unique aspects of the story of the Trans-Mississippi. These aspects include:

- Pre-war theater of political confrontation and terrorism of John Brown
- Texas and the secession referendum
- St. Louis, an unnoticed early strategic victory
- Oklahoma and the Indian nations
- The role of Mexico and Europe in the Trans-Mississippi
- The first invasion of the North
- Naval battles in the Gulf
- Missouri and Arkansas
- The Battle of Galveston
- Dick Dowling and Irish-Catholic heroism at Sabine Pass
- The Red River Campaign
- The Southern exodus to Mexico and South America

Each of these aspects provides a unique and little understood aspect of the events which comprise the division of a nation and war. And in some of these aspects rests an undigested historical event which could have had strategic implications on the war and its final outcome.

As an example, the pre-war days in St. Louis were vital to the first eighteen months of the war. Missouri was a state as likely to secede as to remain in the Union. And had Missouri successfully seceded, the city of St. Louis would have provided a base of operations for Confederate forces to operate against Illinois. Were this reality to be the case in 1861, all the early planning of the war in the West would have been focused on securing the western flank instead of occupying Kentucky. It didn't happen. But the story of why it did not happen demonstrates just how important a relatively minor US Army officer can be in the earliest stages of a political–military event.

The Civil War provides historical events which can be studied in some detail for lessons. The incident in St. Louis is one of those events. However, to my knowledge, it is rarely developed by those who teach this era of American history.

A second element of massive import seldom studied is Mexico and its border with Texas. Colonel "Rip" Ford of Texas, writes in his memoirs about the concerns both South and North had of Mexico as the nation divided. Mexico could have been a mortal threat to Texas or, if properly seduced by President Davis and the Confederacy, could have been a means of bringing Europe into war against the North! Again, this is not a possibility discussed in the routine study of the Civil War.

There are many stories like these about the Trans-Mississippi, stories which would require a student to think, to ponder, to consider.

And there are other stories, ones which excite the imagination and paint a picture of legend and mystic. One of those stories is the Battle of Sabine Pass, Texas, in September 1863. In this battle, a mere 48 Irish-Catholic Texans under the command of Lt. Richard 'Dick" Dowling defeated a Union invading force of 5,000 Yankees in more than 20 ships! It was an astounding victory, one much needed by the South after defeats at Gettysburg and Vicksburg. Sabine Pass is the untold story of an Alamo-like battle where the South defeated all odds driving off the Yankee invaders. There is no comparable battle to this east of the Mississippi River.

The Trans-Mississippi provides a theater of war fresh with new stories, new adventures, new problems for the Civil War student. It is a new place to find the effects of terrorism on the pre-war South. It provides an opportunity to study the political events which led to a public referendum on secession in Texas! (No other state in the South conducted a referendum on secession.)

So as you proceed through the Sesquicentennial, and spend weekends visiting Civil War battlefields and historic locations, consider planning a trip west. What you will find will enhance your understanding of the causes of the war and open your eyes to a different mode of fighting the Civil War.

History seeks a benefactor

Time, historiography, political correctness, and the US government are robbing the South and America of our history.

You could be a person who started out with nothing, and through the grace of God, hard work and opportunity, you earned a fortune. You could be a person who one day went down and bought a lottery ticket which brought you vast sums of money. You could be someone born into a family of great wealth. Whichever you are, if you have a deep love of the South and would like to use your blessings from God for good purpose, than get a cup of coffee, and let's visit awhile.

You see, it's the 150th Anniversary (2010-2015) of the great war over the American Constitution. Most folks call it the Civil War, but there are names much more accurate. The war could have been called the War for Southern Independence, or the War of Lincoln's Conquest. I kind of like the War of the American Constitution because it provides an opportunity for people to consider the origins of the nation, and to study seriously what the Founding Fathers originally meant. And if one does that, then one can see how far the United States has moved from the original confederation of states to what is now a monster, crushing liberty and freedom and promising material equality.

I guess it goes back to my childhood when history teachers would say, "We learn history, so we won't repeat it." Given today's politically correct revisionist interpretations, it is almost certain we will repeat the actual history which occurred, since so few people know what it was!

But, anyway, back to the point of the article.

In the early twentieth century, there were museums all over the South. And since they were financed privately, or commercially, and the story of the Old Confederacy was popular, well, you could find aspects of the real history of the South. You think not? You think I josh? Look at Six Flags Amusement park; the original one in Dallas. How was that park originally set up? By the different flags which flew over Texas: Spain, France, Mexico, the Texas Republic, the United States Flag and the Confederate Flag over the history of the Lone Star state. And the park had a Southern portion (my wife worked in the Civil War Book Store while in college) … though the Southern portion is no longer active. Wouldn't be politically correct, don't you know?

Well, there is history here in Texas little known to the rest of the world, despite the fact the American Civil War is one of the most written about eras in history. You see, most of the war occurred east of the Mississippi River in the areas of Virginia, Kentucky, Tennessee and then into the deep South with Sherman's march to the sea and rape of the Carolinas and Georgia. And of course there was fighting in Louisiana, Alabama, and Mississippi … New Orleans and Vicksburg being two of the most important battles of the war.

But west of the Mississippi, well, that was known as the Trans-Mississippi Theater, a huge vast expanse of America, less populated, less settled. The war in the Trans-Mississippi would be more savage, more personal in some respects. In fact, did you know the pre-war years were dominated by what occurred west of the Mississippi in Kansas and Missouri? Did you know those areas acted as a training ground for terrorism? Sure did.

John Brown, an abolitionist martyr, killed a few folks in the Kansas-Missouri area. He used short swords to slaughter men in front of their wives and children. And no, those men didn't own slaves, just believed it was the law of the land, but that was enough to be butchered by John Brown. Yes, he's the same terrorist who attempted to start a slave revolt at Harper's Ferry.

Well, you can see there are lots of stories to tell here in the Trans-Mississippi. In fact, I wrote an earlier article about the Trans-Mississippi you can read. You might be truly astounded at what you find. You want an example? Well, did you ever hear the story of Dick Dowling and the 47 Irish-Catholics who defeated a Union armada of more than 20 ships and 5,000 Yankees at the Battle of Sabine Pass, Texas, in September 1863? Yes sir, and you know what else? All the Irishmen lived to tell about it. I know … you know the story of the Alamo and

Davy Crockett and Jim Bowie. But almost no one knows the story of Dick Dowling and the Irish!

But that's just one tiny, one-day event, in the great history of the war in the Trans-Mississippi. There's so much more to tell, so go to my earlier article to get a broader view.

Now as far as you, the benefactor, how would we tell this story? Well, sir, (or madame), here's the lowdown!

Ninety miles inside Texas just off Interstate 20, halfway between Shreveport, Louisiana, and Dallas, is Tyler, Texas. Tyler is a beautiful, small American city. For close to a century, she has hosted the Rose Festival, an event of national and international renown. The crowning of the Rose Queen has drawn beautiful young women from New England, Europe and the Middle East. It is one of the most sophisticated and lovely week-long cultural festivals in the entire South. But it's a secret.

Another secret about Tyler is Camp Ford Training and Prisoner of War Camp, Confederate States of America. This was the largest Confederate POW Camp west of the Mississippi. POWs from battles on the Gulf Coast in Louisiana and Arkansas were brought here. Yankee sailors taken from ships operating in the brown-river waters in Louisiana and from the Battle at Sabine Pass were brought here. Men from all over the US Midwest were brought to Camp Ford.

A group from East Texas, the Camp Ford Historical Association, has been working together for decades to raise sufficient monies to build a museum in Tyler. They have made progress, real progress in terms of dollars and facilities purchased. But the vision for the museum is larger than a POW Camp. The vision for this museum is the entire Trans-Mississippi. The story to be told here would encompass tales from California and Oregon to Mexico and the Gulf. Did you know the only Confederate naval victory at sea between a Confederate and federal warship, the CSS *Alabama*, and a Union warship, the USS *Hatteras* occurred off Galveston? There are so many stories and so much of the South to tell. And if we were to find a benefactor or benefactors, we could stay away from federal money and corruptive influence on history which government money brings.

The Camp Ford Historical Association advertises in the *Civil War Magazine*, and has members from all over the nation. About two years back they engaged the Texas Media Group to create three different audio-visual DVD stories about Camp Ford to help promote its history and describe its potential.

The Association engaged an architect to do preliminary design work. This is not a group of people meeting for coffee. Real work has been done. Lee Lawrence, deceased husband of one of the board members, Ann Lawrence, co-authored a book with Dr. Bob Glover about Camp Ford which has been published and is available for purchase.

You could be the person or one of the persons who could make this museum a reality. It could be that God favored you so you could help preserve the true and factual history of the old Confederacy.

America is, or was, a great nation. Its story is full, and a lot of it is either untold or little known. So much is left to be done. If you have been looking for a cause, here is one. You need only search the Camp Ford Historical Association on the Internet if you wish to make contact.

And if you do not possess the wealth to make this a reality, but want to help, we will go the road God has provided for us. If it takes thousands of Americans, tens of thousands of Americans to make this happen, if that's God's plan … than let's get on with it.

Dixie's Greatest Secret

So much written about the South and the War, but in one area, the story has not been told in all its glory. 500 ships, worldwide operations.

The history of the South is replete with stories of daring adventure, bold leadership, matchless courage, and victories against all odds. But the story has been silent on one aspect of the war that could change the view of the sophistication, technological know-how, and international presence of the Confederacy.

The average student of the war and even high school history students know about the battle between the ironclads, the USS *Monitor* and CSS *Virginia*, (often misnamed the *Merrimac*). Of course, the History Channel has covered the recovery of the Confederate submarine CSS *Hunley*. And sometimes, histories of the war will introduce readers to Raphael Semmes and the CSS *Alabama*. But for the most part, we are left thinking the Confederate Navy was little more than a couple of ships.

Before I go further, let me speculate why we are left so completely uninformed on the size, scope and success of the Confederate Navy. I believe it is intentional. I believe it is P.C. (politically correct) to leave the uninformed believing the South was simply not sophisticated enough, educated enough or wise enough to compete with the Yankees. It is P.C. to keep the uninformed thinking the South had no chance, that the Union could never be divided. When one looks at today's omnipotent central government and the absurd policies they impose on 300 million Americans, if Americans realized that secession was a legal, legitimate alternative to the tyranny of Washington, the courts and the president might have to reign in their continuous exercise of power in every aspect of our lives.

One very important way to demonstrate that the war between North and South was much closer than generally acknowledged is to consider the size, scope and operational success of the Confederate Navy. J. Thomas Scharf, father of Confederate Naval history, wrote one of the earliest, if not the first, complete history of the Confederate Navy. *The History of the Confederate States Navy* is more than 800 pages and heavily footnoted. Scharf's work uses a unique set of federal documents and reports, combined with firsthand accounts from Confederate naval personnel.

J. Thomas Scharf attended the Confederate Naval Academy in Richmond in 1863 and served with the Navy through the end of the war. Scharf participated in one of the many special warfare operations conducted by the CS Navy. Scharf spent the rest of his life researching and assembling the South's naval history of the war. The book was published sometime after 1887.

Because Scharf was doing original work immediately after war, his stories often contain factual errors. One must remember sometimes he had only one source for an incident he reported in the book. But his book does provide the ultimate starting point for researching the Southern navy because of its breadth of coverage and the unique collection of reference documents he used to tell the story.

Just some basic surprising about the Confederate Navy to wet your appetite:

a. The Confederate Navy was composed of more than 500 ships!

b. Confederate ironclad squadrons operated in Richmond, Charleston and Mobile.

c. The Confederates built small, iron armored steam powered ships called Davids which were prototype PT boats. They have found records for them in Shreveport and Houston, among other places.

d. Confederate raiders operated all over the world and destroyed the US merchant fleet.

e. CS Naval agents operated in many countries in Europe, purchasing ships and materials and acting as stations to pass on operational orders to Confederate ships docked in European waters.

The Southern navy adds a whole new perspective to the Confederate war effort. Take some time to investigate Dixie's greatest secret!

If you want to pursue this area of the war, visit the Confederate War College, and join as a member. With membership you will be able to download *Clear for Action: an introductory History of the Confederate States Navy*.

⁓ Section VII ⁓

The Confederate Constitution

Answers to today's problems found in third American Constitution!

Democracy ... Southern Style

Answers to today's problems found in third American Constitution!

150 years ago a third Constitution was created in Montgomery, Alabama. The authors foresaw America today and set a course to avoid it.

When first formed, the United States operated under the Articles of Confederation through the Revolutionary War. After the war, the independent nation-states (as recognized by Great Britain's individual treaty with each state) realized changes had to be made to enhance commerce and protection from foreign military adventurism against the infant confederacy. But, when the delegates sent to the convention found it impossible to work with the Articles of Confederation they advised their separate states, and asked to be allowed to draft a new Constitution. The result of their work was the Constitution. However, all states, big and small, North and South retained their right as an independent nation-state to leave the union. Some states like New York, actually articulated this right in the resolution passed by their legislature to rejoin the union under the second constitution! Don and Ron Kennedy co-authors of *The South Was Right!* state clearly in their work; if you cannot leave, you are not free.

In 1860, as a result of conflicting views of national purpose, identity and direction seven Southern states exercised their right to secede, (a right recognized in classes taught at West Point at the time), and met in Montgomery, Alabama, to form another American nation. Later they would be joined by six more states and two territories. The founders of the Confederacy took great pains to make specific changes/modifications to the Constitution they had left to ensure their fears concerning the path the US was taking could be changed. The South would take a very different direction. And despite the present day historical spin of political correctness, a careful reading of the Confederate Constitution and comparison to the US Constitution will clearly illuminate the concerns of the South, and surprisingly demonstrate the men who met in Montgomery in 1860 foretold the problems America faces today!

Before we go further, we must here and now address the question of slavery, as those most frightened by a careful study of the South's governing document will use slavery as the means to distract from the principles important to today's challenges, by attempting to demean and discredit the entire document with sole focus on the peculiar institution. These tacticians of the left are practiced in the art of public discourse, and use distraction as an efficient weapon in the fight for human attention.

Therefore, I state here, and for the record the condemnation of slavery, both as a Southern institution and just as much an institution of the United States and the North. Slavery was the sin of America's nineteenth century just as abortion is the sin of America's twentieth and twenty-first century. With that said, let's look at some of the structural adjustments made by the South to reset the course of their nation to the original course set by the Founders in Philadelphia. The flags of the United States and European nations flew over the slave ships bound for the west. It was not the Confederate Flag. Slaves were spread across all colonies, North and South initially. And it is the US Constitution which did prohibit the slave trade when it was adopted. All but one state in the North had slavery at that time. But in the Southern Constitution, the international slave trade was banned.

There is no means to right this wrong. There is no method to correct the past. But let not those as guilty as we, whitewash the history. In the future, when a time comes where abortion is condemned, it will be the same for those future people. They will be descendants of a barbarous people who slaughtered tens of millions of innocents. This is an aspect of original sin we must learn to use for wiser policy decisions today.

First amongst the changes is found in the Preamble:

WE, the People of the Confederated States, each State acting in its sovereign and independent character, in order to form a permanent Federal government, establish Justice, insure domestic Tranquility and secure the Blessings of Liberty to ourselves and our Posterity, invoking the favor and guidance of Almighty God, do ordain and establish this Constitution for the Confederate States of America.

Inserted in the Preamble are two critical points. Perfection was replaced with permanence. As the South saw it, the threat to the Union came from its oppression and centralization of power. Therefore, permanence, keeping the Union together required a lighter reign, more autonomy on the part of the states. And secondly, God must be invited to the table of governance! Fifty million aborted American souls, most of them from the black community would praise hallelujah to God's guidance in terms of government policy.

In my view, no issue is more important to the election of 2012 than the role of God at the governing table, and the re-establishment of the Christian character of the United States. This is not a new concept, but rather one passed down from the founding. Benjamin F. Morris, a Yankee, wrote a 1,000 page treatise titled *The Christian Life and Character of the Civil Institutions of the United States*. Written in the early years of the War for Southern Independence and published in 1864, this work traces the involvement of Christianity through each phase of the discovery, exploration, settlement and founding of the United States.

The quality of a people, the very nature of a nation revolves around its relationship with God. The decline we see, as a result of the Culture War has done more to bring down America than any war, any depression, any catastrophe endured. President Obama's public pronouncement declaring we are not a Christian nation is the single most important aspect of the 2012 election. No other issue requires more immediate rejection, and reverse.

Extracted from the Preamble was the *joker* of the American Constitution. The card which opened the vast domain of endless power to the central government; "provide for the common defense, promote the general Welfare" The general welfare clause has also been removed from the main body of the Confederate Constitution, thus eliminating a foundational point for law imposed by the Supreme Court through their decisions.

The Confederate founders added value to citizenship; "… no person of foreign birth, and not a citizen of the Confederate States, shall be allowed to vote for any officer, civil or political, State or federal." Further, only citizens could hold office. This provision reduces the incentive to immigrants by removing their right to influence the election of office holders. This is a clear signal to the desire to protect the national character of the South, requiring a generation of assimilation before newcomers could fully be citizens. These policies are quite opposite to today's America, where many attempt to devalue American citizenship by granting rights and privileges to illegal immigrants.

This provision combined with the requirement that a vote of two-thirds of both Houses to raise the president's proposed budget by one dollar set a very high standard for excessive spending, and effectively blocks the creation of the huge deficits presently financing US government operations.

The president is also authorized to use the Line Item Veto: The president may approve any appropriation and disapprove any other appropriation in the same bill. The Southern Constitution grants a lot of power to the executive to run the government, but also limits him/her to one six-year term. The effect of this on spending and budget matters is problematic. How this combination of powers, combined with liberation from re-election syndrome would play out is anybody's guess. In some respects I am fearful of this combination. When we look at presidential executive orders and other actions in the post November months of a president's last term we see immense power unleashed with little restraint.

In an indirect way, the Confederate Constitution prohibits the bailouts of private industries, and or the establishment of laws to affect capitalism and actions of its citizens as consumers; "To regulate Commerce with foreign Nations, and among the several States, and with the Indian Tribes; but neither this, nor any other clause contained in this Constitution, shall ever be construed to delegate the power to Congress to appropriate money for any internal improvement intended to facilitate commerce." This clause could have blocked actions by the Bush and Obama Administrations with respect to bailouts and would also forbid the nationalization of one sixth of the economy, health care.

America did have a second course. Part of the nation attempted to exercise its right to travel that path. These initiatives by the South should be seen as their pre-war anticipation of the Fourteenth Amendment. It might be wise in the Sesquicentennial era to study the alternative route to see if remedies for today's troubles are present in our past.

Democracy Southern Style

"It is the duty of all Nations to acknowledge the providence of Almighty God, to obey his will, to be grateful for his benefits, and humbly to implore his protection and favors."
— George Washington, Thanksgiving Proclamation, 1789

When discussions occur about the South and what *Southern* actually is, those not familiar with the South speak about culture, traditions and history. Hospitality, pretty women, hunting dogs, the Bible, warm summer evenings and hot summer days will almost always be mentioned. Movies like *My Cousin Vinnie* and *Sweet Home Alabama* illustrate the view many Yankees have of the South. Others may focus on the distinct Southern dialects which leave no doubt of Southern origin. And Nashville has kept the idea of the South alive through a wide array of music over the past half century. At some point the description will include slavery and the late war for independence.

Hundreds of thousands of Southern men died defending Dixie and the Southern way of life, and one should wonder exactly what they were fighting for. What caused men to endure four long years of war? Why would men of national reputation and wealth, men like Robert E. Lee and Jefferson Davis sacrifice all they had?

Northerners assert slavery was the sole Southern motive for secession.[5] Yet a surprisingly small amount of Southerners actually owned slaves; so what were all the great majority of non-slave owning Southerners fighting for? Why would these men endure hardships almost unthinkable in today's world, fighting insurmountable odds even after all reasonable hope for victory had been crushed?

It occurred to me that one way to find out what the Southern view of liberty was might be to take a serious look at the Constitution of the Confederate States of America. In this look we will focus on the differences between the Southern Constitution and the one the South left, to see what legal differences might constitute the Southern view of governing. Some very important Southern writers and patriots, including the Kennedy brothers, who wrote the much heralded *The South was Right!*, write they see little difference between the two Constitutions.[6]

---

[5] I believe the constant assertion of slavery as the cause for secession is used to belittle the South's credibility, thus preventing any serious consideration of Southern democratic model and to divert attention from an alternative view of what a democratic society can be.

[6] James and Donald Kennedy, *The South Was Right!* p. 342 "The Constitution of the Confederate States of America was only marginally different from the original United States Constitution." This is not to say that the Kennedy brothers did not identify some significant changes within the CSA Constitution and commend the Montgomery Fathers for their wisdom.

I would offer a very different view. As I spent time with the Constitution drafted in Montgomery, Alabama, I found the Southern statesmen were almost prophetic in identifying the issues and challenges, which would be faced by the United States of America during the twentieth and twenty-first century.

I suggest there are very significant differences between the two documents. Further, I believe that were the Southern Confederacy in existence today, it would be a stronger, more prosperous, more moral nation than our present-day United States of America. Much of today's conservative philosophy, as described by men like Rush Limbaugh and Sean Hannity, seems to have its core in the Southern political philosophy written in the Confederate Constitution of 1861.

A brief review demonstrates at least five major philosophical changes were incorporated by the delegates who met at Montgomery in the spring of 1861:

A restatement of the sovereignty and supremacy of the states *vis-a-vis* the central government supported by changes which shift power away from the central to state governments.[7]

A clear acknowledgement of an all-powerful God as a supreme being. Given the huge majority of Christians within the Confederacy, it seems appropriate to assume the God mentioned is a Christian God.[8]

Additional language protecting the institution of slavery as it existed within the borders of the Confederacy, while prohibiting the further importation of slaves from the US or anywhere else.[9]

An increase in the power of the president *vis-a-vis* the Confederate Congress, particularly with respect to budgetary issues.[10] Growth in central government spending faced significant obstacles because of the requirement for two-thirds majority to increase executive budget bills.

A document which encouraged neither immigration[11] nor domestic industrialization,[12] embracing instead the idea that an open marketplace in Dixie would provide the least expensive goods to the consumer.

This paper will look at exactly that — how did the Constitution of the Confederate States of American differ from the Constitution? And how did those changes reflect the Southern point of view?

To begin with, if the South had been successful in its effort to exercise the right of seces-

---

[7] Preamble
[8] Preamble
[9] Preamble
[10] Article I, Section VII President is given the power of line-item veto. This applies to both legislation and budget bills.
[11] Article I, Section II prohibits foreign born from voting in elections or holding office.
[12] Article I, Section VIII prohibits the expenditure of funds to improve commerce, except for navigational aides on waterways.

sion, one would think the right of secession would be a cornerstone right for the states which joined the CSA.[13] Interestingly the Confederate Constitution clouds the question of secession. Within the Preamble, the Confederates removed the phrase "more perfect union" and replaced it with "a permanent federal government."

The right of secession[14] is possibly the most important Constitutional change which could have occurred as a result of the formation of the Confederate States of America.

If the right to secede was established within the Confederacy, it would establish a *de facto* limit on centralized power, and prevent the rise of an activist judicial branch issuing decrees which have made so much of the controversial law Americans now endure. The Superior Court of the Confederate States would not be in a position to create new law, for should it decide for new law unsupported by the majority of the citizens in the respective states, a state could merely leave. Thus, new law would have to be legislated, meaning it would have to meet the test of securing a majority of representatives. Secession thus becomes the most important tool in limiting the central government.

This one change and the obvious ramifications of the right of secession is the single most important reason for the resuscitation of a peaceful political discussion of the Right of Secession in twenty-first century America. For if secession was once again, as it was in the original union, 15/16 a recognized right of the states, it would go a long way to reimposing real limits on the power of the central government.

This brings us to the second major change, the Preamble to the Constitution of the Confederate States of America invokes "… the favor and guidance of Almighty God …"

The inclusion of a prayer for divine involvement in the governing of the new nation, within the preamble of the Confederate Constitution would make mute forever the argument of separation of church and state which is wrong in its claim with respect to the role of faith in American national governance and politics. The original Founding Fathers clearly wished to prohibit the establishment of a national religion; however, just as clearly, they saw the import of a deep belief in our Almighty God and saw Christianity as the true source of personal

---

[13]Unfortunately, the remaining apparatus of the Union required the South to legitimize the Right of Secession through the force of arms. The overreaching foundational American political axiom that a government should rely on the "consent of the governed" was abandoned in order to sustain Federal authority.

[14]*A View of the Constitution of the United States*, William Rawle used as a textbook at the United States Military Academy, see Appendix to this essay for discussion of the right of secession, which West Pointers studied in the years before the War for Southern Independence.

[15]The Kentucky and Virginia Resolutions, written by Jefferson and Madison, articulated the right of secession and the primacy of the individual states. And it is important to remember that a school text used at the United States Military Academy for at least two decades in the period prior to the Secession Crisis recognized the right of secession.

[16]*A View of the Constitution of the United States*, William Rawle. William Rawle was a friend of George Washington and in his text, which was used at West Point, discussed the right of the states to secede.

liberty. Yet, the forces of Satan have worked hard to separate people from God, and have had their share of success, especially in recent history.

The acknowledgement of the existence of God within our founding governing document instantly places in question a wide array of governmental policies and laws currently in place within the United States: abortion, state lotteries, television and radio programming with indecent material and foul language, while the prohibition against prayer in school could be reversed, and higher standards in social conduct and business ethics could be anticipated.

All of the important standards and values of our nation would look to one source for right and wrong.[17] It is literally impossible to identify all of the changes which would instantly occur in our nation as a result of the acknowledgement of the existence of a Christian God. However, it is reasonable to assume because of the inclusion of the recognition of Almighty God within the Constitution itself, the moral standards of a Confederate nation could be substantially higher than that which exists within the Federalist America today.

The third major change within the Confederate Constitution centers on the relative power between the states and the central government, and between the executive and legislative branches. In general, the Confederate Constitution greatly restricted the power of central government. For example, the Congress was prohibited from passing any law with the purpose of benefiting a specific business or industry! Thus the discussion of a 700 billion dollar bailout of the lending industry in 2009 would be unconstitutional. The South embraced free trade as vitally important to their economy and prohibited within the Constitution actions which might adversely affect that trade, while at the same time allowing funds to be spent for the maintenance of ports, harbors and navigational aids as the only exception to a prohibition of transportation infrastructure spending.

The president was given increased power *vis-a-vis* the Congress, so that he could more effectively control the direction and policies of the government. The chief executive ran for a term of six years, however he was prohibited from re-election. Thus from day one of his presidency, the president need not concern himself with re-election, but rather only with the welfare of his people and nation.

To help him govern, the chief executive was given the power of line-item veto. This power would help to reduce, if not eliminate, the largesse of the individual congressmen and senators. We can assume from this one power either a greatly reduced budget and subsequent need for government revenues and/or taxes or a governing super majority in both Houses of Congress capable of overriding the president's vetoes. In addition, this line-item veto power would enable the president to more tightly control the meaning and authority of each law as it was passed.

---

[17] I recently took a graduate level course in secondary education. Part of the instruction was on classroom ethics. The professor listed on the board ten sources of right and wrong … neither God nor the Bible was mentioned. For me that ended any desire to teach in public institutions. When the teachers are taught wrong, how can the children be taught right?

To further enhance the power of the Executive Branch of government, the Congress was prohibited from spending funds not called for by the heads of the respective executive departments without the support of two-thirds of each house. The Constitution did allow each house to offer to the head of each executive department a non-voting seat on the floor in order to facilitate closer working relations between the two branches.

The Confederate Constitution anticipated many issues which would arise in the decades and centuries to come. The changes may reflect issues which had already arisen by the time of its writing, but clearly it lays down a different vision of government, one which is much more restrained. Southerners, then as now, do not look upon government as the great problem solver, but rather as a device required by the necessities of life. The authors of the Confederate Constitution saw, as did the original writers of the Federal Constitution, that the greatest real threat to individual liberty came from our own government. And they saw the danger of integrating the needs of business and industry into the role of the central government. They also saw the great danger of ambitious congressmen and senators, who, for their own purposes, have turned the annual budget into Christmas for the special interests smart enough to invest in a residence in or near the national capital. They rightly balanced the electoral needs of the legislature with a single-term president given sufficient powers to reign in parochial interests and to steer the ship of state in terms of policy and spending.

When one studies the Southern Constitution, it seems clear the war was about preserving the freedoms won in the American Revolution: Limits on centralized power, sustainment of the primacy of state sovereignty, continuance of slavery, a rejection of modern industrialization, building an economy on an agricultural base, and relying on trade to provide for the manufactured goods needed by the Southern people. It seems clear Southerners saw a direct connection between economics and politics, more specifically that political liberty is a commodity, which is best protected by limiting population growth and rejecting commercial concentration in cities. For Southerners, it appears they saw their freedom in the land, and in lower population densities.

Appendix 1: Notes concerning West Point text citing right to secede

Source: *Jefferson Davis*, by Herman S. Frey, Frey Enterprises, 605 Merritt Street, Nashville, TN 37203, 1977 and 1978

A View of the Constitution of the United States, William Rawle, textbook used by Chaplain C. P. Rawle, instructor at West Point during Jefferson Davis' years as cadet:

"If a fraction should attempt to subvert the government of a state for the purpose of destroying its republican form, the paternal power of the Union could thus be called forth to subdue it.
"Yet it is not to be understood, that its interposition would be justifiable, if the people of a state should determine to retire from the Union … It depends on the state itself … whether it will continue a member of the Union. To deny this right would be inconsistent with the principle on which all our political system is founded, which is, that the people have in all cases, a right to determine how they will be governed … The states, then, may wholly withdraw from the Union … secession of a state from the Union depends on the will of the people of such state."

While the above quotation and the source being a textbook at the United States Military Academy, clearly indicates the sovereignty of the respective states and the will of the people with respect to the form of government to be in place … it is self evident from American history and from our own revolution against the British Empire that our nation was founded on inherent authority of the governed to select its government. Further, since the thirteen colonies voluntarily joined the Union, and since the Constitution itself, through the Bill of Rights, reserved all powers not delineated in the Constitution to the people and the states respectively, it is clear the national sovereignty rose from the people, through the respective states to the central government.

The failure of the federal government to conduct a trial against President Davis after the war and the warnings of the sitting Supreme Court Justice against such a trial make it clear secession was not illegal.

The Constitution of the Confederate States of America

WE, the People of the [**United States**] *__Confederated States, each State acting in its sovereign and independent character,__* in order to form a [**more perfect Union**] *__permanent Federal government,__* establish Justice, insure domestic Tranquillity [provide for the common defense, promote the general Welfare], and secure the Blessings of Liberty to ourselves and our Posterity, *__invoking the favor and guidance of Almighty God,__* do ordain and establish this Constitution for the [**United**] *Confederate* States of America.

ARTICLE I

SECTION I

All legislative Powers herein [granted] *delegated,* shall be vested in a Congress of the [**United**] *__Confederate__* States, which shall consist of a Senate and House of Representatives.

SECTION II

The House of Representatives shall be composed of Members chosen every second Year by the People of the several States, and the Electors in each State shall *__be citizens of the Confederate States, and__* have the Qualifications requisite for Electors of the most numerous Branch of the State Legislature; *__but no person of foreign birth, and not a citizen of the Confederate States, shall be allowed to vote for any officer, civil or political, State or federal.__*

No Person shall be a Representative who shall not have attained to the Age of twenty-five Years, and [**been seven Years a Citizen of the United**] *__be a citizen of the Confederate__* States, and who shall not, when elected, be an Inhabitant of that State in which he shall be chosen.

Representatives and direct Taxes shall be apportioned among the several States which may be included within this [**Union**] *__Confederacy,__* according to their respective Numbers, which shall be determined by adding to the whole Number of free Persons, including those bound to Service for a Term of Years, and excluding Indians not taxed, three-fifths of all [**other Persons**] *__slaves__*. The actual Enumeration shall be made within three Years after the first Meeting of the Congress of the [**United**] *__Confederate__* **States,** and within every subsequent Term of ten Years, in such Manner as they shall by Law direct. The Number of Representatives shall not exceed one for every [**thirty**] *__fifty__* Thousand, but each State shall have at Least one Representative; and until such enumeration shall be made, the State of [**New Hampshire shall be entitled to chuse three, Massachusetts eight, Rhode Island and Providence Plantations one, Connecticut five, New York six, New Jersey four, Pennsylvania eight, Delaware one, Maryland six, Virginia ten, North Carolina five, South Carolina five, and Georgia three**] *__South Carolina shall be entitled to choose six, the State of Georgia ten, the State of Alabama nine, the State of Florida two, the State of Mississippi seven, the State of Louisiana six, and the State of Texas six.__*

When vacancies happen in the Representation from any State, the Executive Authority thereof shall issue Writs of Election to fill such Vacancies.

The House of Representatives shall choose their Speaker and other Officers; and shall have the sole Power of Impeachment; *except that any judicial or other federal officer resident and acting solely within the limits of any State, may be impeached by a vote of two-thirds of both branches of the Legislature thereof.*

SECTION III

The Senate of the [**United**] *__Confederate__* States shall be composed of two Senators from each State, chosen by the Legislature thereof, for six Years, **_at the regular session next immediately preceding the commencement of the term of service;_** and each Senator shall have one Vote.

Immediately after they shall be assembled in Consequence of the first Election, they shall be divided as equally as may be into three Classes. The Seats of the Senators of the first Class shall be vacated at the Expiration of the second Year, of the second Class at the Expiration of the fourth Year, and of the third Class at the Expiration of the sixth Year, so that one-third may be chosen every second Year; and if Vacancies happen by Resignation, or otherwise, during the Recess of the Legislature of any State, the Executive thereof may make temporary Appointments until the next Meeting of the Legislature, which shall then fill such Vacancies.

No Person shall be a Senator who shall not have attained to the Age of thirty Years, and [**been nine Years a Citizen of the United**] **_be a citizen of the Confederate_** States, and who shall not, when elected, be an Inhabitant of that State for which he shall be chosen.

The Vice President of the [**United**] *__Confederate__* States shall be President of the Senate, but shall have no Vote, unless they be equally divided.

The Senate shall chose their other Officers, and also a President pro tempore, in the Absence of the Vice President, or when he shall exercise the Office of President of the United States.

The Senate shall have the sole Power to try all Impeachments. When sitting for that Purpose, they shall be on Oath or Affirmation. When the President of the [**United**] *__Confederate__* States is tried, the Chief Justice shall preside: And no Person shall be convicted without the Concurrence of two-thirds of the Members present.

Judgment in Cases of Impeachment shall not extend further than to removal from Office, and Disqualification to hold and enjoy any Office of honour, Trust or Profit under the **[United]** **_Confederate_** States; but the Party convicted shall nevertheless be liable and subject to Indictment, Trial, Judgment and Punishment, according to Law.

SECTION IV

The Times, Places and Manner of holding Elections for Senators and Representatives, shall be prescribed in each State by the Legislature thereof, **_subject to the provisions of this Constitution;_** but the Congress may at any time by Law make or alter such Regulations, except as to the **_times and_** places of chusing Senators.

The Congress shall assemble at least once in every Year, and such Meeting shall be on the first Monday in December, unless they shall by Law appoint a different Day.

SECTION V

Each House shall be the Judge of the Elections, Returns and Qualifications of its own Members, and a Majority of each shall constitute a Quorum to do Business; but a smaller Number may adjourn from day to day, and may be authorized to compel the Attendance of absent Members, in such Manner, and under such Penalties as each House may provide.

Each House may determine the Rules of its Proceedings, punish its Members for disorderly Behaviour, and, with the Concurrence of two-thirds **_of the whole number_** expel a Member.

Each House shall keep a Journal of its Proceedings, and from time to time publish the same, excepting such Parts as may in their Judgment require Secrecy; and the Yeas and Nays of the Members of either House on any question shall, at the Desire of one-fifth of those Present, be entered on the Journal

Neither House, during the Session of Congress, shall, without the Consent of the other, adjourn for more than three days, nor to any other Place than that in which the two Houses shall be sitting.

SECTION VI

The Senators and Representatives shall receive a Compensation for their Services, to be ascertained by Law, and paid out of the Treasury of the **[United]** <u>**Confederate**</u> States. They shall in all Cases, except Treason [Felony] and Breach of the Peace, be privileged from Arrest during their Attendance at the Session of their respective Houses, and in going to and returning from the same; and for any Speech or Debate in either House, they shall not be questioned in any other Place.

No Senator or Representative shall, during the Time for which he was elected, be appointed to any civil Office under the Authority of the **[United]** <u>**Confederate**</u> States, which shall have been created, or the Emoluments whereof shall have been encreased during such time; and no Person holding any Office under the **[United]** <u>**Confederate**</u> States, shall be a Member of either House during his Continuance in Office. <u>**But Congress may, by law, grant to the principal officers in** each of the executive departments a seat upon the floor of either House, with the privilege of discussing any measures appertaining to his department.</u>

SECTION VII

All Bills for raising Revenue shall originate in the House of Representatives; but the Senate may propose or concur with Amendments as on other Bills.

Every Bill which shall have passed [the House of Representatives and the Senate] _both Houses,_ shall, before it becomes a Law, be presented to the President of the [United] _Confederate_ States; If he approves he shall sign it, but if not he shall return it, with his Objections to that House in which it shall have originated, who shall enter the Objections at large on their Journal, and proceed to reconsider it. If after such Reconsideration two-thirds of that House shall agree to pass the Bill, it shall be sent, together with the Objections, to the other House, by which it shall likewise be reconsidered, and if approved by two-thirds of that House, it shall become a Law. But in all _such_ Cases the Votes of both Houses shall be determined by Yeas and Nays, and the Names of the Persons voting for and against the Bill shall be entered on the Journal of each House respectively. If any Bill shall not be returned by the President within ten Days (Sundays excepted) after it shall have been presented to him, the Same shall be a law, in like Manner as if he had signed it, unless the Congress by their Adjournment prevent its return, in which Case it shall not be a Law. _**The President may approve any appropriation and disapprove any other appropriation in the same bill. In such case he shall, in signing the bill, designate the appropriation disapproved, and shall return a copy of such appropriation, with his objections, to the House in which the bill shall have originated; and the same proceedings shall then be had as in case of other bills disapproved by the President.**_

Every Order, Resolution, or Vote to which the Concurrence of [the Senate and House of Representatives] _both Houses_ may be necessary (except on a question of Adjournment), shall be presented to the President of the [United] _Confederate_ States; and before the Same shall take Effect, shall be approved by him, or being disapproved by him, [shall] _may_ be repassed by two-thirds of [the Senate and House of Representatives] _both Houses,_ according to the Rules and Limitations prescribed in the Case of a Bill.

SECTION VIII

The Congress shall have Power

To lay and collect Taxes, Duties, Imposts and *Excises, for revenue necessary* to pay the Debts [and], provide for the common Defence [and general Welfare of the United States; but], **_and carry on the government of the Confederate States; but no bounties shall be granted from the treasury, nor shall any duties, or taxes, or importation from foreign nations be laid to promote or foster any branch of industry; and_** all Duties, Imposts and Excises shall be uniform throughout the [United] **_Confederate_** States;

To borrow Money on the credit of the [United] **_Confederate_** States;

To regulate Commerce with foreign Nations, and among the several States, and with the Indian Tribes; **_but neither this, nor any_** other clause contained in this Constitution, shall ever be construed to delegate the power to Congress to appropriate money for any internal **_improvement intended to facilitate commerce; except for the purpose of furnishing lights, beacons, and buoys, and other aids to navigation upon the coasts, and the improvement of harbors, and the removing of obstructions in river navigation; in all such cases such duties shall be laid on the navigation facilitated thereby, as may be necessary to pay the costs and expenses thereof;_**

To establish a uniform Rule of Naturalization, and uniform Laws on the subject of Bankruptcies throughout the [United] **_Confederate_** States; **_but no law of Congress shall discharge any debt contracted before the passage of the same;_**

To coin Money, regulate the Value thereof, and of foreign Coin, and fix the Standard of Weights and Measures;

To provide for the Punishment of counterfeiting the Securities and current Coin of the [United] *Confederate* States;

To establish Post Offices and post [Roads] *routes; but the expenses of the Post Office Department, after the first day of March, in the year of our Lord eighteen hundred and sixty-three, shall be paid out of its own revenues;*

To promote the progress of Science and useful Arts, by securing for limited Times to Authors and Inventors the exclusive Right to their respective Writings and Discoveries;

To constitute Tribunals inferior to the supreme Court;

To define and punish Piracies and Felonies committed on the high Seas, and Offences against the Law of Nations;

To declare War, grant Letters of Marque and Reprisal, and make Rules concerning Captures on Land and Water;

To raise and support Armies, but no Appropriation of Money to that Use shall be for a longer Term than two Years;

To provide and maintain a Navy;

To make Rules for the Government and Regulation of the land and naval Forces;

To provide for calling forth the Militia to execute the Laws of the [Union] *Confederate States*, suppress Insurrections and repel Invasions;

To provide for organizing, arming, and disciplining the Militia and for governing such Part of them as may be employed in the Service of the [United] *Confederate* States, reserving to the

States respectively, the Appointment of the Officers, and the Authority of training the Militia according to the Discipline prescribed by Congress;

To exercise exclusive Legislation in all Cases whatsoever, over such District (not exceeding ten Miles square) as may, by Cession of particular States, and the Acceptance of Congress, become the Seat of the Government of the **[United]** *Confederate* States, and to exercise like Authority over all Places purchased by the Consent of the Legislature of the State in which the Same shall be, for the Erection of Forts, Magazines, Arsenals, Dock-Yards, and other needful Buildings;--And

To make all Laws which shall be necessary and proper for carrying into Execution the foregoing Powers, and all other Powers vested by this Constitution in the Government of the **[United]** *Confederate* States or in any Department or Officer thereof.

SECTION IX

[The Migration or Importation of such Persons as any of the States now existing shall think proper to admit, shall not be prohibited by the Congress prior to the Year one thousand eight hundred and eight, but a Tax or Duty may be imposed on such Importation, not exceeding ten dollars for each Person.] *The importation of negroes of the African race from any foreign country other than the slaveholding States or territories of the United States of America, is hereby forbidden; and Congress is required to pass such laws as shall effectually prevent the same. Congress shall also have power to prohibit the introduction of slaves from any State not a member of, or territory not belonging to, this Confederacy.*

The Privilege of the Writ of *Habeas Corpus* shall not be suspended, unless when in Cases of Rebellion or Invasion the public Safety may require it. No Bill of Attainder or ex post facto Law, **_or law denying or impairing the right of property in negro slaves_**, shall be passed.

No Capitation, or other direct, Tax shall be laid, unless in Proportion to the Census or Enumeration hereinbefore directed to be taken.

No Tax or Duty shall be laid on Articles exported from any State, **_except by a vote of two-thirds of both Houses._**

No Preference shall be given by any Regulation of Commerce or Revenue to the Ports of one State over those of another [**:nor shall Vessels bound to, or from, one State, be obliged to enter. clear, or pay Duties in another**].

No Money shall be drawn from the Treasury, but in Consequence of Appropriations made by Law; and a regular Statement and Account of the Receipts and Expenditures of all public Money shall be published from time to time.

Congress shall appropriate no money from the Treasury except by a vote of two-thirds of both Houses, taken by yeas and nays, unless it be asked and estimated for by some one of the heads of departments and submitted to Congress by the President; or for the purpose of paying its own expenses and contingencies; or for the payment of claims against the Confederate States, the justice of which shall have been officially declared by a tribunal for the investigation of claims against the Government, which it is hereby made the duty of Congress to establish.

All bills appropriating money shall specify in Federal currency the exact amount of each appropriation and the purposes for which it is made; and Congress shall grant no extra

<u>compensation to any public contractor, officer, agent or servant, after such contract shall have been made or such service rendered.</u>

No Title of Nobility shall be granted by the [**United**] <u>**Confederate**</u> **States;** and no Person holding any Office of Profit or Trust under them, shall, without the Consent of the Congress, accept of any present, Emolument, Office, or Title, of any kind whatever, from any King, Prince or foreign State.

Congress shall make no law respecting an establishment of religion, or prohibiting the free exercise thereof; or abridging the freedom of speech, or of the press; or the right of the people peaceably to assemble, and to petition the Government for a redress of grievances.

A well regulated Militia, being necessary to the security of a free State, the right of the people to keep and bear Arms shall not be infringed.

No Soldier shall, in time of peace, be quartered in any house, without the consent of the Owner, nor in time of war, but in a manner to be prescribed by law.

The right of the people to be secure in their persons, houses, papers, and effects, against unreasonable searches and seizures, shall not be violated, and no Warrants shall issue, but upon probable cause, supported by Oath or affirmation, and particularly describing the place to be searched, and the persons or things to be seized.

No person shall be held to answer for a capital, or otherwise infamous crime, unless on a presentment or indictment of a Grand Jury, except in cases arising in the land or naval forces, or in the Militia, when in actual service in time of War or public danger; nor shall any person be subject for the same offence to be twice put in jeopardy of life or limb; nor shall be compelled in any Criminal Case to be a witness against himself, nor be deprived of life, liberty or property without due process of law; nor shall private property be taken for public use, without just compensation.

In all criminal prosecutions, the accused shall enjoy the right to a speedy and public trial, by an impartial jury of the State and district wherein the crime shall have been committed, which district shall have been previously ascertained by law, and to be informed of the nature and cause of the accusation; to be confronted with the witnesses against him; to have Compulsory process for obtaining Witnesses in his favour, and to have the Assistance of Counsel for his defence.

In Suits at common law, where the value in controversy shall exceed twenty dollars, the right of trial by jury shall be preserved, and no fact tried by a jury shall be otherwise reexamined in any Court of the [**United**] <u>*Confederate*</u> States, than according to the rules of the common law.

Excessive bail shall not be required, nor excessive fines imposed, nor cruel and unusual punishments inflicted.

<u>***Every law or resolution having the force of law, shall relate to but one subject, and that shall be expressed in the title.***</u>

SECTION X

No State shall enter into any Treaty, Alliance, or Confederation; grant Letters of Marque and Reprisal; coin Money; [**emit Bills of Credit;**] make any Thing but gold and silver Coin a Tender in Payment of Debts; pass any Bill of Attainder, *or* ex post facto Law, or Law impairing the Obligation of Contracts, or grant any Title of Nobility.

No State shall, without the consent of the Congress, lay any Imposts or Duties on Imports or

Exports, except what may be absolutely necessary for executing its inspection Laws: and the net Produce of all Duties and Imposts, laid by any State on Imports or Exports, shall be for the Use of the Treasury of the **[United]** _Confederate_ States; and all such Laws shall be subject to the Revision and Control of the Congress.

No State shall, without the Consent of Congress, lay any Duty of Tonnage, _**except on sea-going vessels, for the improvement of its rivers and harbors navigated by the said vessels; but such duties shall not conflict with any treaties of the Confederate States with foreign nations; and any surplus of revenue thus derived shall, after making such improvement, be paid into the common treasury; nor shall any State**_ keep Troops, or Ships of War in time of Peace, enter into any Agreement or Compact with another State, or with a foreign Power, or engage in War, unless actually invaded, or in such imminent Danger as will not admit of Delay. _**But when any river divides or flows through two or more States, they may enter into compacts with each other to improve the navigation thereof.**_

ARTICLE II

SECTION I

[The executive Power shall be vested in a President of the United States of America. He shall hold his Office during the Term of four Years, and, together with the Vice President, chosen for the same Term, be elected, as follows:] _The executive power shall be vested in a President of the Confederate States of America. He and the Vice President shall hold their offices for the term of six years; but the President shall not be re-eligible. The President and Vice President shall be elected as follows:_

Each State shall appoint in such Manner as the Legislature thereof may direct, a Number of

Electors, equal to the whole Number of Senators and Representatives to which the State may be entitled in the Congress; but no Senator or Representative, or Person holding an Office of Trust or Profit under the [**United**] *__Confederate__* States, shall be appointed an Elector.

The Electors shall meet in their respective States, and vote by ballot for President and Vice President, one of whom, at least, shall not be an inhabitant of the same State with themselves; they shall name in their ballots the person voted for as President, and in distinct ballots the person voted for as Vice President, and they shall make distinct lists of all persons voted for as President, and of all persons voted for as Vice President, and of the number of votes for each, which lists they shall sign and certify, and transmit sealed to the seat of the government of the [**United**] *__Confederate__* States, directed to the President of the Senate;—The President of the Senate shall, in presence of the Senate and House of Representatives, open all the certificates and the votes shall then be counted;--The person having the greatest number of votes for President shall be the President, if such number be a majority of the whole number of Electors appointed; and if no person have such majority, then from the persons having the highest numbers not exceeding three on the list of those voted for as President, the House of Representatives shall choose immediately, by ballot, the President. But in choosing the President, the votes shall be taken by States, the representation from each State having one vote; a quorum for this purpose shall consist of a member or members from two-thirds of the States, and a majority of all the States shall be necessary to a choice. And if the House of Representatives shall not choose a President whenever the right of choice shall devolve upon them, before the fourth day of March next following, then the Vice President shall act as President, as in the case of the death or other constitutional disability of the President. The person having the greatest number of votes as Vice President shall be the Vice President, if such number be a majority of the whole number of Electors appointed, and if no person have a majority, then from the two highest numbers on the list the Senate shall choose the Vice President; a quorum for the purpose shall consist of two-thirds of the whole number of Senators, and a majority of the whole number shall be necessary to a choice. But no person constitutionally ineligible to the office of President shall be eligible to that of Vice President of the [**United**] *Confederate* States.

The Congress may determine the Time of choosing the Electors, and the Day on which they shall give their Votes; which Day shall be the same throughout the United States.

No Person except a natural born Citizen [**or a Citizen of the United States**] *of the Confederate States, or a citizen thereof,* at the time of the Adoption of this Constitution, *or a citizen thereof born in the United States prior to the 20th of December, 1860,* shall be eligible to the Office of President; neither shall any Person be eligible to that Office who shall not have attained to the Age of thirty-five Years, and been fourteen Years a Resident within the [**United States**] *limits of the Confederate States, as they may exist at the time of his election.*

In Case of the Removal of the President from Office, or of his Death, Resignation, or Inability to discharge the Powers and Duties of the said Office, the same shall devolve on the Vice President, and the Congress may by Law provide for the Case of Removal, Death, Resignation, or Inability, both of the President and Vice President, declaring what Officer shall then act as President, and such Officer shall act accordingly, until the Disability be removed, or a President shall be elected.

The President shall, at stated Times, receive for his Services, a Compensation, which shall neither be increased nor diminished during the Period for which he shall have been elected, and he shall not receive within that Period any other Emolument from the [**United**]

**Confederate** States or any of them.

Before he enters on the Execution of his Office, he shall take the following Oath or Affirmation:

"I do solemnly swear (or affirm) that I will faithfully execute the Office of President of the [**United**] _**Confederate**_ States, and will to the best of my Ability, preserve, protect and defend the Constitution [**of the United States**] _thereof._"

SECTION II

The President shall be Commander in Chief of the Army and Navy of the [**United**] _**Confederate**_ States, and of the Militia of the several States, when called into the actual Service of the [**United**] _**Confederate**_ States; he may require the Opinion, in writing, of the principal Officer in each of the executive Departments, upon any Subject relating to the Duties of their respective Offices, and he shall have Power to grant Reprieves and Pardons for Offences against the [**United**] _**Confederate**_ States, except in Cases of Impeachment.

He shall have Power, by and with the Advice and Consent of the Senate, to make Treaties, provided two-thirds of the Senators present concur; and he shall nominate, and by and with the Advice and Consent of the Senate, shall appoint Ambassadors, other public Ministers and Consuls, Judges of the supreme Court, and all other Officers of the [**United**] _**Confederate**_ States, whose Appointments are not herein otherwise provided for, and which shall be established by Law: but the Congress may by Law vest the Appointment of such inferior Officers, as they think proper, in the President alone, in the Courts of Law, or in the Heads of Departments. _**The principal officer in each of the executive departments, and all persons connected with the diplomatic service, may be removed from office at the pleasure of the**_

President. All other civil officers of the executive department may be removed at any time by the President, or other appointing power, when their services are unnecessary, or for dishonesty, incapacity, inefficiency, misconduct, or neglect of duty; and when so removed, the removal shall be reported to the Senate, together with the reasons therefore.

The President shall have Power to fill **[up]** all Vacancies that may happen during the Recess of the Senate, by granting Commissions which shall expire at the End of their next Session.

SECTION III

[He] *The President* shall from time to time give to the Congress Information of the State of the **[Union]** *Confederacy,* and recommend to their Consideration such Measures as he shall judge necessary and expedient; he may, on extraordinary Occasions, convene both Houses, or either of them, and in Case of Disagreement between them, with Respect to the Time of Adjournment, he may adjourn them to such Time as he shall think proper; he shall receive Ambassadors and other public Ministers; he shall take Care that the Laws be faithfully executed, and shall Commission all the officers of the **[United]** *Confederate* States,

SECTION IV

The President, Vice President and all civil Officers of the **[United]** *Confederate* States, shall be removed from Office on Impeachment for, and Conviction of, Treason, Bribery, or other high Crimes and Misdemeanors.

ARTICLE III

SECTION I

The judicial Power of the [**United**] *__Confederate__* States shall be vested in one [**supreme**] *__Superior__* Court, and in such inferior Courts as the Congress may from time to time ordain and establish. The Judges, both of the supreme and inferior Courts, shall hold their Offices during good Behavior, and shall, at stated Times, receive for their Services a Compensation, which shall not be diminished during their Continuance in Office.

SECTION II

The judicial Power shall extend to all cases [**in Law and Equity, arising under this Constitution**], *__arising under this Constitution, in law and equity,__* the Laws of the [**United**] *__Confederate__* States, and Treaties made, or which shall be made, under their Authority;- to all Cases affecting Ambassadors, other public Ministers, and Consuls;—to all Cases of admiralty and maritime Jurisdiction;—to Controversies to which the [**United**] *__Confederate__* States shall be a Party; —to Controversies between two or more States;--between a State and Citizens of another State *__where the State is plaintiff ;—between__* **Citizens** *__claiming lands under grants__* of different' States**,—**[**between Citizens of the same State claiming Lands under Grants of different States,**] and between a State, or the Citizens thereof, and foreign States, Citizens or Subjects; *__but no State shall be sued by a citizen or subject of any foreign State.__*

In all Cases affecting Ambassadors, other public Ministers and Consuls, and those in which a State shall be Party, the supreme Court shall have original Jurisdiction. In all the other Cases before mentioned, the supreme Court shall have appellate Jurisdiction, both as to Law and Fact, with such Exceptions, and under such Regulations as the Congress shall make.

The Trial of all Crimes, except in Cases of Impeachment, shall be by Jury; and such Trial shall be held in the State where the said Crime[s] shall have been committed; but when not committed within any State, the Trial shall be at such Place or Places as the Congress may by Law have directed.

SECTION III

Treason against the **[United]** *<u>Confederate</u>* States shall consist only in levying War against them, or in adhering to their Enemies, giving them Aid and Comfort. No Person shall be convicted of Treason unless on the Testimony of two Witnesses to the same overt Act, or on Confession in open Court.

The Congress shall have Power to declare the Punishment of Treason, but no Attainder of Treason shall work Corruption of Blood, or Forfeiture except during the Life of the Person attainted.

ARTICLE IV

SECTION I

Full Faith and Credit shall be given in each State to the public Acts, Records, and judicial Proceedings of every other State. And the Congress may by general Laws prescribe the Manner in which such Acts, Records and Proceedings shall be proved, and the Effect thereof.

SECTION II

The Citizens of each State shall be entitled to all Privileges and Immunities of Citizens in the several States, ***<u>and shall have the right of transit and sojourn in any State of this Confederacy, with their slaves and other property; and the right of property in such slaves</u>***

shall not be impaired.

A Person charged in any State with Treason, Felony, or other Crime, who shall flee from Justice, and be found in another State, shall on Demand of the executive Authority of the State from which he fled, be delivered up, to be removed to the State having Jurisdiction of the Crime.

No *slave or* Person held to Service or Labour in [**one State**] *any State or Territory of the Confederate States* under the Laws thereof, escaping *or unlawfully carried* into another, shall, in Consequence of any Law or Regulation therein, be discharged from such Service or Labour, but shall be delivered up on Claim of the Party to whom such *slave belongs, or to whom such* Service or Labour may be due.

SECTION III

[**New States may be admitted by the Congress into this Union;**] *Other States may be admitted into this Confederacy by a vote of two-thirds of the whole House of Representatives and two-thirds of the Senate, the Senate voting by States*; but no new State shall be formed or erected within the Jurisdiction of any other State; nor any State be formed by the Junction of two or more States, or Parts of States, without the Consent of the Legislatures of the States concerned as well as of the Congress.

The Congress shall have Power to dispose of and make all needful Rules and Regulations [**respecting the Territory or other Property belonging to the United States; and nothing in this Constitution shall be so construed as to Prejudice any Claims of the United States, or of any particular State**] *concerning the property of the Confederate States, including the lands thereof.*

The Confederate States may acquire new territory, and Congress shall have power to legislate and provide governments for the inhabitants of all territory belonging to the Confederate States lying without the limits of the several States, and may permit them, at such times and in such manner as it may by law provide, to form States to be admitted into the Confederacy. In all such territory the institution of negro slavery as it now exists in the Confederate States shall be recognized and protected by Congress and by the territorial government, and the inhabitants of the several Confederate States and territories shall have the right to take to such territory any slaves lawfully held by them in any of the States or Territories of the Confederate States.

SECTION IV

The [**United**] *Confederate* States shall guarantee to every State [**in this Union**] *that now is, or hereafter may become, a member of this Confederacy,* a Republican Form of Government, and shall protect each of them against Invasion; and on Application of the Legislature, or of the Executive (when the Legislature [**cannot be convened**] *is not in session)* against domestic Violence.

ARTICLE V

[**The Congress, whenever two-thirds of both Houses shall deem it necessary, shall propose Amendments to this Constitution, or on the Application of the Legislatures of two-thirds of the several States, shall call a Convention for proposing Amendments, which, in either Case, shall be valid to all Intents and Purposes, as Part of this Constitution, when ratified by the Legislatures of three-fourths of the several States, or by Conventions in three-fourths thereof, as the one or the other Mode of Ratification may be proposed by** the Congress; Provided that no Amendment which may be made prior to the Year one thousand eight hundred and eight shall in any Manner affect the first and fourth Clauses in the Ninth Section of the first Article; and that no State, without its Consent, shall be deprived of its equal Suffrage in the Senate.]

Upon the demand of any three States, legally assembled in their several Conventions, the Congress shall summon a Convention of all the States, to take into consideration such amendments to the Constitution as the said States shall concur in suggesting at the time when the said demand is made; and should any of the proposed amendments to the Constitution be agreed on by the said Convention—voting by States—and the same be ratified by the Legislatures of two-thirds of the several States, or by Conventions in two-thirds thereof—as the one or the other mode of ratification may be proposed by the general Convention—they shall henceforward form a part of this Constitution. But no State shall, without its consent, be deprived of its equal representation in the Senate.

ARTICLE VI

The Government established by this Constitution is the successor of the Provisional Government of the Confederate States of America, and all laws passed by the latter shall continue in force until the same shall be repealed or modified; and all the officers appointed by the same shall remain in office until their successors are appointed and qualified or the offices abolished.

All Debts contracted and Engagements entered into, before the Adoption of this Constitution, shall be as valid against the [**United**] *Confederate* States under this Constitution, as under the [**Confederation**] *Provisional Government*.

This Constitution and the Laws of the [**United**] *__Confederate__* States [**which shall be**] made in Pursuance thereof; and all Treaties made, or which shall be made, under the authority of the [**United**] *__Confederate__* States, shall be the supreme Law of the Land; and the Judges in every State shall be bound thereby, any Thing in the Constitution or Laws of any State to the Contrary notwithstanding.

The Senators and Representatives before mentioned, and the Members of the several State Legislatures, and all executive and judicial Officers, both of the [**United**] *__Confederate__* States and of the several States, shall be bound by Oath or Affirmation, to support this Constitution; but no religious Test shall ever be required as a Qualification to any Office or public Trust under the [**United**] *__Confederate__* States.

The enumeration in the Constitution, of certain rights, shall not be construed to deny or disparage others retained by the people *__of the several States.__*

The powers not delegated to the [**United**] *__Confederate__* States by the Constitution, nor prohibited by it to the States, are reserved to the States respectively, or to the people.

ARTICLE VII

The Ratification of the Conventions of [**nine**] *five* States, shall be sufficient for the Establishment of this Constitution between the States so ratifying the same.

__When five States shall have ratified this Constitution, in the manner before specified, the Congress under the Provisional Constitution shall prescribe the time for holding the election of President and Vice President; and for the meeting of the electoral college; and for counting the votes and inaugurating the President. They shall also prescribe the time for holding the__ *first election of members of Congress under this Constitution, and the time for assembling the same. Until the assembling of such Congress, the Congress under the Provisional Constitution shall continue to exercise the legislative powers granted them, not extending beyond the time limited by the Constitution of the Provisional Government.*

[DONE in Convention by the Unanimous Consent of the States present the Seventeenth Day of September in the Year of our Lord one thousand seven hundred and Eighty seven and of the Independence of the United States of America the Twelfth.]

Adopted unanimously March 11, 1861.

Source: *The Confederate Military History*, Appendix to Volume 12

Remember when America was made of heroes?

Would your organization like to meet one?

The American Civil War is full of stories of heroes and adventure. Hidden away in the pages of Texas history is a story about a young man who led a group of Irish-Catholic-Texans in a desperate fight against overwhelming odds.

Born Richard O' Dowling, in County Galway, Ireland, Dick led an adventurous life from the very beginning. Sailing as a young lad from Ireland to America with his family, he saw America first through the bustling streets of America's busiest port, New Orleans.

Listen to Mark as he portrays Dick and tells his story up to the most important morning of his life.

On September 8, 1863, at a place called Sabine Pass on the coast of Texas, a fleet of twenty-eight federal ships, carrying 5,000 Federals sailed towards a small fort with only six guns and less than fifty Irish-Texans. What happened that morning shook the world and a legend more astonishing than the Alamo was born..

Mark Vogl, a graduate of The Citadel and former Army infantry officer, portrays the spirit of Major Dick Dowling, the commander of the forty-eight men who stood firm to oppose the Yankee fleet.

Mark is a practiced storyteller who has visited with groups from Orlando to Houston and all across the South. An author and historian, he is often invited back.

$500 plus travel and lodging will insure an evening of delight.

Fees are negotiable depending on the size of the group.

Contact Mark at 903-725-3175

The Rebel Mountain Story Teller

Mark K. Vogl

Does your camp or organization need a storyteller?

Mark has given presentations in thirteen states to scores of groups and thousands of people interested in the history of the Confederacy! Mark Vogl is a graduate of The Citadel, former Army combat arms officer, college professor, political aide and author.

Mark's first book, *Military Lessons of the Civil War*, was published in the spring of 2007 and received the Jefferson Davis Historical Gold Medal from the United Daughters of the Confederacy. His second book, published early in 2008, *The Rebel Mountain Reader*, is a book which includes many of the presentations listed below and more.

Mark is the great-great-grandson of Private David Parks Walter, 33rd North Carolina Volunteers, part of the famed Lane's Brigade, Stonewall Jackson's Corps, Army of Northern Virginia. A former member of the Sons of Confederate Veterans since 1994, Mark was awarded the Texas Division Confederate of the Year Award in 2009. He served as the 2nd Lt. Commander and Lt. Commander of the Texas Division.

Mark can make presentations as a Confederate Infantry captain serving in a North Carolina regiment, as a Southern statesman/civilian or in jacket and tie. Mark has developed a number of formal presentations, but would be open to developing one especially for your organization given sufficient time. You can choose from the presentations listed below or he can craft a story just for your group.

Available presentations include:

History

Jackson and the Valley Campaign
In the spring of 1862, the most lethal combination of commanders in the war would first join to devise and execute a strategy to assist General Joseph Johnston in defense of Richmond. Together, Lee as the military adviser to President Davis and General Jackson as commander of the District of the Shenandoah, would develop a strategy studied to this day!

The Life of Dick O'Dowling
Major Dick Dowling, CSA, (born O'Dowling in Tuam, Ireland) commanded the forty-eight Texans who successful fought off 5,000 Yankees at Sabine Pass. This presentation is done in the first person … let Dick O' Dowling, himself, tell about his life.

A View from Seminary Ridge
A formal presentation that discusses the reasons for General Lee's decision to conduct Pickett's Charge on the third day at Gettysburg. This presentation features a large full color, three-dimensional replica of the Gettysburg battlefield.

Dixie's Greatest Secret
Supported by overhead projector and slides, this presentation focuses on the size, scope and success of the Confederate Navy.

"I will pay that sum" Robert E. Lee, a Bicentennial Presentation of the Man and the Christian
This presentation is based on the written words of R.E. Lee himself, his youngest son, Captain Robert E. Lee, CSA, and his nephew, General Fitzhugh Lee, CSA. It is intended to introduce the real Marse Robert, the man.

The Red River Campaign 1864
This presentation discusses why the campaign was conducted, and the general outline of the campaign. Strategic aspects of the campaign are the central parts of this talk.

Texas and the War for Southern Independence
Discusses ten different aspects of the War as it relates to Texas. Usually given to school children.

Jefferson Davis, American Patriot, American President
A look at Jeff Davis and some startling facts you may not know about the South's wartime leader.

Confederate Christmas
This presentation focuses on Christmas in the Confederacy during the years 1860 through 1865.

Christmas in the Confederate White House
Taken from Varina Davis' story published in *The New York World* newspaper in 1896.

Democracy, Southern Style
The Confederate Constitution is significantly different from the Federal Constitution anticipating many modern-day issues.

Current Events & Politics

The Southern Movement
This presentation speaks to a wide array of organizations, individuals, educational and commercial enterprises involved in promoting Southern traditions and values.

Southern Fried Ramblings
This presentation provides a brief overview of the book released through Amazon Kindle.

The Confederate War College
This presentation focuses on the website www.confederatewarcollege.com, and its purpose, success and activities.

The Right Path
This is a presentation that focuses on Mark's vision of the reforms necessary to make the Texas Division and the Sons of Confederate Veterans a combat effective unit in the Culture War. This presentation is not for the faint of heart.

Contact Information: Mark Vogl, PO Box 825, Gilmer, Texas 75644-0825, johnyreb43@yahoo.com, 903-725-3175

www.ingramcontent.com/pod-product-compliance
Lightning Source LLC
Chambersburg PA
CBHW080411300426
44113CB00015B/2484